The Master's Plan for the Church

from the bible-teaching ministry of

Charles R. Swindoll

INSIGHT FOR LIVING

The Master's Plan for the Church

INSIGHT FOR LIVING

Charles R. Swindoll graduated in 1963 from Dallas Theological Seminary, where he now serves as the school's fourth president, helping to prepare a new generation of men and women for the ministry. Chuck has served in pastorates in three states: Massachusetts, Texas, and California, including almost twenty-three years at the First Evangelical Free Church in Fullerton, California. He is currently senior pastor of Stonebriar Community Church in Frisco, Texas, north of Dallas. His sermon messages have been aired over radio since 1979 as the *Insight for Living* broadcast. A best-selling author, he has written numerous books and booklets on many subjects.

Based on the outlines and transcripts of Charles R. Swindoll's sermons, the study guide text was developed and written by the Pastoral Ministries Department at Insight for Living.

Editor in Chief:
Cynthia Swindoll

Study Guide Writer:
Jason Shepherd

Senior Editor and Assistant Writer:
Wendy Peterson

Assistant Editor:
Glenda Schlahta

Editors:
Karla Lenderink
Christianne Varvel

Rights and Permissions:
The Meredith Agency

Text Designer:
Gary Lett

Graphic System Administrator:
Bob Haskins

Director, Communications Division:
John Norton

Print Production Manager:
Don Bernstein

Project Coordinator:
Jennifer Hubbard

Printer:
Sinclair Printing Company

Unless otherwise identified, all Scripture references are from the New American Standard Bible, updated edition, copyright © The Lockman Foundation 1960, 1962, 1963, 1968, 1971, 1972, 1973, 1975, 1977, 1995. Used by permission. Scripture taken from the Holy Bible, New International Version, Copyright © 1973, 1978, 1984 International Bible Society, used by permission of Zondervan Bible Publishers [NIV].

An effort has been made to locate sources and obtain permission where necessary for the quotations used in this book. In the event of any unintentional omission, a modification will gladly be incorporated in future printings.

ISBN 1-57972-349-7

Cover design: Scott Littlejohn

Cover images: (from left) © 2000 Marc Romanelli/The Image Bank; © 2000 Eyewire; © 2000 Roy Gumpel/Stone Images; © 2000 Photodisc

Printed in the United States of America

CONTENTS

INTRODUCTION

What is the church all about, anyway?

It's not about the faddish, the new, the cute, or the clever. The church is eternal, built on timeless principles, and is designed to showcase the radiant, redeeming love of Jesus Christ.

It's not a dated institution, a steepled structure, or a commercial money-making machine. The church is people who are called to be on fire for God, to draw others into the circle of the Spirit's renewing warmth and light.

It's not big business, a slick corporation, or a political precinct. The church is a family, or as Paul put it, "the household of God," which was originated to be "the pillar and support of the truth" (1 Tim. 3:15).

Jesus said of His church, "The gates of Hades will not overpower it" (Matt. 16:18)—something He never said about anything else.

Why, then, do so many churches look overpowered and undernourished? Why do so many lose their distinctiveness in an effort to be trendy? Why do some abuse rather than edify? Or squander people's trust through the misuse of money? Or dilute the gospel of Jesus Christ to keep attendance numbers growing?

They've lost track of the Master's plan for His church.

In this study, I want to refocus our attention on the Chief Architect's design. I want to blow the dust off God's inspired blueprint and revitalize God's people for God's purposes. Join me, won't you, as we learn about the Master's exciting plan for the church— and find fresh instruction on how to live it out!

Chuck Swindoll

Charles R. Swindoll

PUTTING TRUTH
INTO ACTION

Knowledge apart from application falls short of God's desire for His children. He wants us to apply what we learn so that we will change and grow. This study guide was prepared with these goals in mind. As you go through the following pages, we hope your desire to discover biblical truth will grow as your understanding of God's Word increases, and that you will be encouraged to apply what you've learned.

To assist you in your study, we've included a section called **Living Insights** at the end of each lesson. These exercises will challenge you to study further and to think of specific ways to put your discoveries into action.

There are many ways to use this guide—in personal devotions, group studies, discussions with friends and family, and Sunday school classes. And, of course, it's an ideal study aid when you're listening to its corresponding *Insight for Living* radio series.

To benefit most from this study guide, we would encourage you to consider it a spiritual journal. That's why we've included space in the **Living Insights** for recording your thoughts and discoveries. We hope you'll return to those sections often for review and encouragement as you continue to grow in your walk with Christ.

Insight for Living

Chapter 1

THE CHURCH: LET'S DO IT RIGHT THIS TIME

2 Timothy 2:1–7

There's no such thing as "the perfect church"—a single model or ideal to which all local churches should conform. Every body of believers, by God's own design, should embrace a unique statement of faith, style of worship, and way of witnessing to its community. There is, however, such a thing as the perfect *plan* for the church.

God's plan for the church—contained within the pages of the Bible—offers many valuable guidelines and standards to help maximize our efforts in every area of congregational life, from service and evangelism to elder boards and spiritual leadership. Whatever specific model a local church decides to follow, it can wrap its distinctives around God's unchanging design for Christ's body.

Who better to begin our discussion of the Master's plan with than the apostle Paul, a man whose life and work has had more impact on the church than any other human, except Jesus Himself? But let's not watch Paul at the beginning of his ministry, when his hopes and dreams were untried. Let's catch him at the end, after they had been put through the crucible of reality and had proved to be steady and true—after he had logged thousands of miles in ministry, endured innumerable beatings for the faith, and witnessed Christianity at its finest (the Romans and Thessalonians) and its worst (the Corinthians).

Paul's second letter to Timothy was written at the end of his ministry. It was, in fact, the last of all his writings. He penned it from a dungeon cell beneath the city streets of first-century Rome when he was "being poured out as a drink offering," and the time of his departure had come (2 Tim. 4:6).

Because Paul fought the good fight, finished the course, and kept the faith (v. 7), his advice on church life is invaluable to us. So let's look at his final instructions to Timothy. From these instructions we'll discover the three pillars that undergird the Master's plan for the church—the three practices that every church must perform to ensure that it's giving its best. After all, only our best will build Christ's kingdom and bring glory to God.

Strong in Grace

Paul wasted no time in getting to his first point.

> You therefore, my son, be strong in the grace that is in Christ Jesus. (2 Tim. 2:1)

There's no mistake that Paul was writing to an individual—his protégé, Timothy. And there is no doubt that the apostle's words must be taken personally, that each of us must strive to apply his instructions to our individual lives. But if each member of a church exhibits the qualities stated here, won't the whole body exemplify these qualities as well? So Paul's words apply to church as well as to individual believers.

The first pillar of a godly church is grace. Paul knew that few qualities can make a church winsome and refreshing the way grace can. It can breathe life into any assembly. His words encourage us to stand strong in that grace—literally, "be strengthened within"— so that we will reflect grace in our attitudes and actions toward one another. One way to accomplish this is to live in freedom, giving each other room to grow through failures and mistakes.

Perhaps another reason Paul wanted us to stand strong in grace is that there's no greater enemy to a church than legalism. The best way to strangle a growing community is to force its members to fulfill to the letter what some consider to be a set of essential standards. That's legalism. More specifically, it's marked by a rigid attitude of strict conformity to someone else's requirements in order to gain acceptance and respect. Christ said that His yoke is easy and His burden is light. Let's not weigh it down with a load of petty demands.

We can't be strong in grace on our own. It takes relying on *God's* strength, which comes only through the power of the Holy Spirit who indwells us. God Himself does through us what He requires of us and our churches.

Committed to Discipleship

Next, Paul wrote,

> The things which you have heard from me in the presence of many witnesses, entrust these to faithful men, who will be able to teach others also. (v. 2)

Paul used the word *entrust* here as a commercial term, referring to the way a bank guards the money entrusted to it. Applied to spiritual teaching, *entrusting* does not refer to locking the teaching of Scripture away in some vault, but to keeping an eye on its purity and thereby protecting it from falsehood and heresy.[1] The idea is that churches should entrust the teaching of God's truth to members who will keep it safe—pure and undefiled.

How can we tell who is worthy of such trust? Paul said to look for people who are faithful. Barclay expands on this term:

> The Greek for faithful, *pistos*, is a word with a rich variety of closely connected meanings. A man who is a *pistos* is a man who is *believing*, a man who is *loyal*, a man who is *reliable*. All these meanings are there. . . . These believing men are such "that they will yield neither to persecution nor to error." The teacher's heart must be so stayed on Christ that no threat of danger will lure him from the path of loyalty and no seduction of false teaching causes him to stray from the straight path of the truth. He must be steadfast alike in life and in thought.[2]

Paul had already entrusted God's Word to Timothy. He wanted Timothy to deposit it into the lives of others, and he wanted those disciples to pass it on to others in an ever-multiplying transaction of discipleship. The same holds true for churches today. God wants us to commit ourselves to making disciples, but only disciples who will be true to the sacred trust that was given to them to teach the Word accurately and clearly.

---

1. Philip H. Towner, *1–2 Timothy and Titus*, the IVP New Testament Commentary Series (Downers Grove, Ill.: InterVarsity Press, 1994), p. 170.

2. William Barclay, *The Letters to Timothy, Titus, and Philemon*, The Daily Bible Study Series (Philadelphia, Penn.: Westminster Press, 1975), p. 158.

Faithful through Hardship

The third and final pillar of a godly church is faithfulness through hardship. Paul used three images to help us understand exactly what this kind of loyalty looks like.

Like a Soldier

Paul first said that church members must prepare themselves to remain faithful during hardship—the way soldiers prepare for war:

> Suffer hardship with me, as a good soldier of Christ Jesus. No soldier in active service entangles himself in the affairs of everyday life, so that he may please the one who enlisted him as a soldier. (vv. 3–4)

In keeping themselves ready for war, soldiers employ single-minded devotion to their cause and the one who enlists them. They refuse to entangle themselves in civilian affairs because it would impede their ability to fight and win if an invasion occurred. Maintaining this level of readiness requires unwavering discipline. When Paul wrote to Timothy, he had the Roman soldiers in mind—men who had perfected the art. Josephus offers this description of the Roman military:

> Each soldier every day throws all his energy into his drill, as though he were in action. Hence that perfect ease with which they sustain the shock of battle: no confusion breaks their customary formation, no panic paralyzes, no fatigue exhausts them. All their camp duties are performed with the same discipline, the same regard for security: the procuring of wood, food-supplies, and water, as required—each party has its allotted task; nothing is done without a word of command. The same precision is maintained on the battlefield; nothing is done unadvisedly or left to chance. This perfect discipline makes the army an ornament of peace-time and in war welds the whole into a single body; so compact are their ranks, so alert their movements, so quick their ears for orders, their eyes for signals, their hands to act upon them. None are slower than they in succumbing to suffering.[3]

3. Josephus, *Wars of the Jews,* as quoted by Philip H. Towner, *1–2 Timothy and Titus,* p. 172.

Wow! What would our churches look like if we gave ourselves to the cause of Christ the way the Roman soldiers served their empire? If we did, our local assemblies would be like the Roman army—slow in succumbing to suffering. No hardship would break us from formation, no disagreement would cause dissension in our ranks, and no enemy would weaken our resolve. In other words, the gates of hell would never prevail against us.

This level of readiness, however, comes only from faithfulness forged by discipline. We must be eternally vigilant to make sure that we're not involving ourselves in the ways of the world or accepting the world's values.

Like an Athlete

Athletes, like soldiers, exhibit devotion and discipline:

> Also if anyone competes as an athlete, he does not win the prize unless he competes according to the rules. (v. 5)

Notice the specific point Paul drew out concerning athletes: they don't win unless they play by the rules. At first, it sounds like Paul was referring to obedience to the stipulations of lawful behavior—a runner must stay in his lane, a wrestler must not step outside the circle, and so on. But a closer examination of the text reveals a different meaning. Barclay notes,

> There is a very interesting point in the Greek here which is difficult to bring out in translation. . . . The Greek is *athlein nomimōs*. In fact that is the Greek phrase which was used by the later writers to describe a *professional* as opposed to an *amateur* athlete. The man who strove *nomimōs* was the man who concentrated everything on his struggle. His struggle was not just a spare-time thing, as it might be for an amateur; it was a whole-time dedication of his life to excellence in the contest which he had chosen. Here then we have the same idea as in Paul's picture of the Christian as a soldier. A Christian's life must be concentrated upon his chosen contest. The spare-time Christian is a contradiction in terms; a man's whole life should be an endeavour to live out his Christianity.[4]

4. William Barclay, *The Letters to Timothy, Titus, and Philemon*, p. 161.

For the believer, playing by the rules doesn't mean living by a list of dos and don'ts. Rather, it means living up to the standard of wholehearted service to God and His people.

While not all churches are called to suffer to the same degree, the same level of devotion still has its place. It allows us to give and serve when we're tired, to come together when the circumstances oppose it, and to hope in God when difficult situations arise. And if we finish the race as Paul did, we'll stand before Christ, step up to the podium, and receive the medal of His approval—which is more precious than pure gold!

Like a Farmer

Finally, Paul gave us his third image—the image of a farmer:

> The hard-working farmer ought to be the first to receive his share of the crops. (v. 6)

Farmers' lives are full of hard, back-breaking work—and this only describes the lives of farmers today, men and women who live in our post-industrial revolution, high-technology age. The agrarians in Paul's day had no tractors or harvesters; they didn't even have hand tools made out of lightweight metals. They literally toiled for every grain or grape or olive they harvested.

Want to know what it takes for a church to remain faithful during hard times? Consider the efforts of the ancient farmer. Faithfulness today is no more easily achieved. When churches suffer, conflicts arise. People get snippy and snappy—they get on each other's nerves and jump down each other's throats. To remain unified, we must toil to make sure that all disputes are dealt with thoroughly and quickly, allowing no conflict to go unresolved. No, it's neither easy nor pleasant, but toiling does have its rewards.

Paul promised us that we will partake in the benefits of our efforts, just as a farmer receives a share of his crops, just as a disciplined soldier achieves victory, and just as a devoted athlete wins a crown. What is our prize? We'll receive the privilege of watching God change the lives and save the souls of the people in our neighborhoods, communities, and across the globe as a result of our hard work.

In conclusion, Paul exhorted his readers and gave another promise:

> Consider what I say, for the Lord will give you understanding in everything. (v. 7)

The word *consider* means "to perceive in the mind." Consider what Paul has said about the three pillars of a godly church: grace, discipleship, and faithfulness. They are the supports upon which we will construct the rest of the Master's plan for the church. Without them, the plan is like a roof sitting flat on the ground—nice to look at but not worth much. So take time to consider what God has said. If you do, God promises to give you understanding.

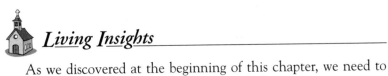

Living Insights

As we discovered at the beginning of this chapter, we need to apply Paul's words to our personal lives before we can integrate them into our communal lives. And this makes sense—change in the church happens one person at a time. With this in mind, let's examine ourselves under the light of God's words.

In what ways do you exhibit hints of legalism by holding people to standards or expectations that are not explicitly worded in Scripture?

_____

_____

_____

Based on your answer, now grade yourself on how well you show grace toward others: A   B   C   D   F

How can you raise your grade? Specifically, in what ways do you need to relax?

_____

_____

Now consider the area of discipleship. Howard Hendricks often says, "Every believer needs a Paul, a Timothy, and a Barnabas." In other words, everyone needs a mentor, disciple, and best friend. Do you currently have all three? If not, write down the names of people with whom you'd like to pursue these kinds of relationships:

Mentor: _____

Disciple: _____

Friend: _____

Describe a time when you had to endure a hardship.

_____

_____

_____

_____

In what ways did you exhibit the readiness of a soldier, the devotion of an athlete, and the hard work of a farmer?

_____

_____

_____

_____

The next time suffering comes your way, what will you do to be even more godly in your attitudes and actions?

_____

_____

_____

_____

Chapter 2

THE CHURCH: WHAT IS ABSOLUTELY ESSENTIAL?

Acts 2:42–47

It's pop-quiz time! Clear your desk, take out a pen or pencil, and circle the answer or answers that correctly complete the sentence below.

The *top priorities* of a church should be . . .

A. to amass a large number of weekly attendees or participants.

B. to build an impressive physical plant with a large campus and beautiful buildings and landscaping.

C. to conform to the most popular style of worship.

D. to subscribe to a specific form of church government such as "elder-rule" or "congregation-rule."

E. to make sure that at least 20 percent of the annual budget goes to missions.

F. to engage in politics by endorsing candidates and marching in demonstrations.

G. None of the above.

Which options did you circle? The only correct answer is "G. None of the above." Remember, the question asked only for the *top priorities* of the church. Some of the items listed in A–F are important, and a couple of them are *very* important, but they're not *top priorities*.

After taking a test or quiz, no matter how well you did, it always helps to go back to the class notes or textbook to look up the answers.

Parts of this chapter are adapted from "Our Objectives" and "A Genuine Concern for Others" in the Bible study guide *The Bride: Renewing Our Passion for the Church*, written by Gary Matlack, from the Bible-teaching ministry of Charles R. Swindoll (Anaheim, Calif.: Insight for Living, 1994) and from "Spiritual Pediatrics" in the Bible study guide *The Birth of an Exciting Vision: A Study of Acts 1:1–9:43*, written by Bryce Klabunde, from the Bible-teaching ministry of Charles R. Swindoll (Anaheim, Calif.: Insight for Living, 1992).

So let's turn to our text, the Bible, and discover where the top priorities of the church are found and what God says about them.

Four Essentials for the Church

Perhaps the clearest statement of the church's priorities is located in the book of Acts, chapter 2. And why shouldn't it be? Acts 2 records the birth of the church. After describing Pentecost and Peter's sermon, which brought approximately 3,000 people to faith in Christ, the author Luke told us about life in the newly-formed body:

> They were continually devoting themselves to the apostles' teaching and to fellowship, to the breaking of bread and to prayer. (Acts 2:42)

The first thing we notice about these new believers is that they were "devoted" members of the church. The term *devoted, proskartereō,* connotes a "steadfast and single-minded fidelity to a certain course of action."[1] They gave themselves wholeheartedly to their new faith and their new church.

Exactly how did the early believers devote themselves to their church? By participating in the four basic facets—the top priorities —of church life. Let's take a closer look at each one.

Learning

First, *they were devoted to the apostle's teaching.* Why do you suppose teaching is the first item listed in the order of activities? Because no matter where believers are in their spiritual development, they need sustenance to grow and keep growing. Babies need milk; adults need meat—the Bible supplies both.

The apostles considered the ministry of God's Word to be of primary importance. In fact, they thought it was so important that they delegated their other duties so that they could focus only on teaching (see Acts 6:1–6). The demands of their fledgling ministry were great, but as important as those needs were, their primary task was that of feeding the flock.

The ministry of the Word is no less important today. It begins, of course, with the Gospel, and we rejoice when lost sheep come into

1. Richard N. Longnecker, "The Acts of the Apostles," *The Expositor's Bible Commentary,* ed. Frank E. Gaebelein (Grand Rapids, Mich.: Zondervan Publishing House, Regency Reference Library, 1981), vol. 9, p. 289.

the fold. But if they hear *only* the Gospel week after week, they become infirm and atrophied, lacking the strength for daily living in Christ. Instead, they need a steady diet of the rest of God's Word.

Consider the benefits of consistent, biblical teaching and preaching:

- It gives substance to our faith.

- It stabilizes us in times of testing.

- It enables us to handle God's Word correctly.

- It equips us to detect and confront false teaching.

- It makes us confident in our walk.

- It calms our fears and cancels our superstitions.

A word of caution here: learning is only one of the church's priorities. Elevating it at the sacrifice of the others creates churches with smug academic atmospheres. When knowledge remains theoretical, it breeds indifference. When it disregards love and grace, it leads to intolerance. When it becomes an end in itself, it fosters idolatry. Remember what Paul said in 1 Corinthians 8:1b, "Knowledge makes arrogant, but love edifies." And that leads us to the next priority of the church: love.

Loving

It's no wonder that God blessed the new church with growth. In addition to Peter's powerful sermons, they had a community filled with love and acceptance—something that's hard to resist in the middle of a cold, cruel world.

The early Christians would have had a hard time relating to the modern-day custom of sitting inconspicuously in church, then slipping out the back door during the closing prayer. They gathered not only to sing songs and listen to sermons, but to be with one another, to care for and share with one another. They came for love—the second of the top priorities, which comes through fellowship.

The Greek word for "fellowship," *koinōnia*, signifies a close relationship. Its root, *koinos*, means "common" or "communal."2 The

2. Walter Bauer, *A Greek-English Lexicon of the New Testament and Other Early Christian Literature*, 2nd ed. Revised and augmented by F. Wilbur Gingrich and Frederick W. Danker, from Walter Bauer's 5th ed., 1958 (Chicago, Ill.: University of Chicago Press, 1979), pp. 438–39.

early church was a close, sharing group. That's the idea of Acts 2:44:

> And all those who had believed were together and
> had all things in common.

It's sad to think how many Christians today are missing the kind of closeness the first Christians shared. Sermons and songs, while uplifting and necessary, provide only part of a vital church encounter. We need involvement with others as well.

The New Testament portrays true fellowship in two primary ways. First, it paints it as an act of sharing something tangible to meet a need. Note verse 45:

> And they began selling their property and posses-
> sions and were sharing them with all, as anyone
> might have need.

What a picture of sacrificial giving! Believers were selling land and personal belongings not for personal gain, but to help each other. That's one form of fellowship. The other form comes in the shape of shared experience—weeping with those who weep, rejoicing with those who rejoice, grieving with those who grieve. Sometimes the best gift we can give is ourselves. Who can assign a dollar value to the tears we shed for someone else's loss? Or the time we give to listen to someone vent his or her frustration? Or our applause upon learning of a friend's accomplishment?

Koinōnia. Fellowship. Love. It happens when God's people come together in the spirit of sharing, when full hands and hearts reach out to fill empty ones. Then the body of Christ is strengthened. And hopefully, the world takes notice.

Worshiping

The new believers also devoted themselves to worship. Like an irresistible perfume, the holy fragrance of their worship wafted to God, and as a result, all of them "kept feeling a sense of awe" (Acts 2:43a). The Greek reads, "and fear came to every soul." This was more than music-induced goosebumps or "warm fuzzies" from a sermon. Their worship carried them into the very presence of God, and they were overcome with the magnificence of His holiness.

Does this mean they worked themselves into mindless frenzies? Absolutely not, but neither did they sit in rigid, emotionless formality. Verse 46 tells us that

> day by day continuing with one mind in the temple, and breaking bread from house to house, they were taking their meals together with gladness and sincerity of heart

(literally, "simplicity of heart"), which erupted in praise to God (v. 47). That's just what worship is: a human response—involving both heart and mind—to divine revelation. And when it happens, God is pleased, because He delights in genuine worshipers (John 4:23).

The early church, while avoiding chaos, effervesced with the spontaneous expression of heartfelt worship. Unfortunately, many churches today have replaced genuine worship with soulless rituals, heartless lectures, or mindless extravaganzas. Ask yourself if your church fits this description:

> In many (most?) churches there are programs and activities . . . but so little worship. There are songs and anthems and musicals . . . but so little worship. There are announcements and readings and prayers . . . but so little worship. The meetings are regular, but dull and predictable. The events are held on time, led by well-meaning people, supported by folks who are faithful and dedicated . . . but that tip-toe expectancy and awe-inspiring delight mixed with a mysterious sense of the fear of almighty God are missing.[3]

One thing is for sure—the early church definitely did not fit this description. They devoted themselves to the genuine worship of God.

Praying

Finally, the new believers devoted themselves to prayer. The Greek literally reads, "They were continually devoting themselves to *the prayers*." It implies they gathered together, as a standard practice, for the primary purpose of praying corporately to God.

We shouldn't be surprised that these prayer meetings became such a high priority for the new Christians. They kindled the believers toward personal involvement with one another and sparked

---

3. Charles R. Swindoll, *The Bride: Renewing Our Passion for the Church* (Grand Rapids, Mich.: Zondervan Publishing House, 1994), p. 40 (page citation is to the second printing).

a passion to know and serve the Lord. They also enabled the Christians to listen to and care for each other in the most profound way.

As the book of Acts progresses, it reveals what an integral part prayer played in the life of the early church (compare 4:24; 6:4; 12:5; 13:3; and 20:36). The same holds true today. Prayer, in fact, is the only link we have to Christ as we carry out His work here on earth. It's the only way in which we can receive His guidance and strength.[4]

Like the earliest Christians, we, too, can experience a kindling effect when we pray for other believers, when we join with them in prayer. On the other hand, however, if we isolate ourselves, we'll become like a charred ember that falls from the fire, slowly growing cold and dark.

Has our discussion of the four priorities taken you by surprise? If it has, you're not alone. Many churches have become distracted by less important things. Some have lost themselves in the details—focusing on rules, procedures, and protocol. Others have become enticed by the signs of success—big numbers and impressive facilities. And still others have lost their way by obsessing over one or two areas of church life, such as missions or small groups. True success, however, goes to the church that keeps at the top of its list learning, love, worship, and prayer—and keeps them in balance.

 Living Insights

The four priorities we've discussed in this chapter are generally regarded as four separate areas of church life, but a case can be made for viewing them as four elements of a single gathering.[5] With this in mind, take a few minutes to reflect on how well your church balances the four priorities in its Sunday morning services. Under each of the following categories, jot down the specific activities it performs or makes available in that area.

Teaching _____

_____

4. Also refer to Acts 4:29–30; 6:6; 8:15; 14:23; 28:8.

5. I. Howard Marshall, *The Acts of the Apostles*, The Tyndale New Testament Commentaries Series (Grand Rapids, Mich.: William B. Eerdmans Publishing Company, 1992), p. 83.

_____

_____

Fellowship _____

_____

_____

_____

_____

Worship _____

_____

_____

_____

_____

Corporate Prayer _____

_____

_____

_____

_____

Which categories do you feel are over-emphasized?

_____

How can the church pare down or eliminate some activities to bring these areas back into proportion?

_____

_____

_____

_____

_____

Which categories are under-emphasized?

_____

How can the church expand or create new activities to bolster these areas?

_____

_____

_____

_____

_____

It's often surprising how open pastors and church leaders can be to suggestions from the congregation, especially when those suggestions are given in the right spirit and through the proper channels. Write the names of people in your church who are responsible for the church's Sunday morning activities.

_____

Now, choose one of these people and write out the suggestion you'd like to present to him or her.

_____

_____

_____

_____

_____

Finally, make an appointment to speak to this person and start praying for your time together. Remember, _everyone_ in the early church was devoted to the church's activities. If you don't give your input, you're essentially robbing the church of a precious resource. By the way—be ready to give of your own time and energy to turn your suggestions into reality if the church leader proves to be open to them. After all, it wouldn't be fair to bring all your great ideas and expect someone else to make them happen, would it?

Chapter 3

WHO IS QUALIFIED
TO LEAD THE CHURCH?

1 Timothy 3:1–2

Death had crept over the Pride Lands like a gray-green shadow. The ground, once covered with a mane of windswept grass and spotted with wild blossoms, now had the look of reptile skin shed and left to dry and crack under the African sun. Brittle branches, the only remnants of vegetation, jutted from the parched land like lifeless claws. The earth, once rumbling under galloping hooves of antelope and wildebeest, was silent now, strewn with skulls and bones picked clean by hungry hyenas.

One lion was responsible for this desolation—Scar. He had usurped the throne by murdering his brother, King Mufasa, and driving Simba, the king's son and rightful heir, away from Pride Rock. And he had given free reign to the bitter enemies of Mufasa, the hyenas, allowing these trespassing scavengers to roam and ravage the countryside—their reward for helping Scar kill the king.

From a cliff on the outskirts of the Pride Lands, Simba, now a full-grown lion, scowled as he surveyed what was left of his homeland. The real king had at last returned. And it was time to take Pride Rock back. To do that, he must challenge Scar . . .

This story, of course, is told in Walt Disney's record-breaking movie, *The Lion King*. The film reveals an important truth about leadership: At the top, character matters. Though Scar had the title of king, he didn't qualify for the position. He used the throne to feed his appetite for power and position rather than to protect and care for his kingdom.

Abusive and irresponsible leadership thrives in the real world too. And unfortunately, it exists in the body of Christ. Insecure and manipulative pastors and elders have ravaged congregations and split churches. Some can't control their own passions. Others care more about success than people.

Parts of this chapter are adapted from "Checklist for Choosing Church Leaders" in the Bible study guide *Excellence in Ministry: A Study of 1 Timothy*, written by Gary Matlack, from the Bible-teaching ministry of Charles R. Swindoll (Anaheim, Calif.: Insight for Living, 1996).

17

No matter what your position in the church—whether you're a leader yourself or in any way responsible for choosing them—you need to know the biblical qualifications. Fortunately, Paul gave them to us in 1 Timothy 3:1–7. His checklist, if followed, will help us choose the right leaders for our churches.

Two Basic Facts concerning Church Leaders

Before we study Paul's list, let's look at two basic facts concerning church leadership.

Qualified Leadership Balances Two Extremes

The operative term here is *qualified*. Over the course of history, the pendulum of power has swung to two extremes. At times, church leaders have seized power and used it to control, manipulate, and abuse the laity. At other times, however, the laity have unjustifiably rejected the leadership of good men, failing to show the proper respect for authority. Neither extreme pleases God. *Qualified* leadership occurs when righteous men serve their flock wisely and selflessly and are supported by their congregations.

Selecting Leaders Is Not to be Done by Voting

Church leaders are not selected by voting; they're appointed. "What?!" you say. "That's downright un-American!" And you're right. But we are Christians first, Americans second. The Bible frequently clashes with our culture, as much as we'd like to think otherwise. But if church leaders are not to be selected democratically, how are they to be chosen?

While the Bible doesn't give us specific instructions, it does provide a model. In Acts, when the church was first being formed, the elders and pastors were hand-picked by the disciples (14:23). Later, in Titus, we see this practice continued as the existing body of leadership chose the new leaders (1:5).

Note, however, that the appointing was done by men who were spiritually mature themselves, and even then the choices were made only after much fasting and prayer.

God's Checklist of Qualifications

But who is qualified to be a leader in the church? 1 Timothy 3:1–7 gives us a checklist to follow, but first, let's look at two contextual considerations.

First, we need to understand that this list applies to male candidates for the office of pastor or elder. Not that women don't or shouldn't demonstrate many of these same qualities, but Scripture indicates that only men should hold this office. In chapter 2, we're told that men are to be the spiritual leaders of the church (vv. 8, 12). And the requirements for being "the husband of one wife" (3:2a) and a manager of "his own household" (v. 4a) imply that Paul had men in mind.

Second, we need to know that these qualifications are essential, not optional. Note the imperative, "An overseer . . . *must*" (v. 2; see also vv. 4, 7). This passage presents a standard for leaders, not a pool of qualities from which to skim and pick. To qualify, an individual must meet all the criteria.

Paul organized his list into four main categories, revealing the necessary well-roundedness that every overseer must possess. He addressed the man's personal life (vv. 1–3), his domestic life (vv. 4–5), his church life (v. 6), and his public life (v. 7). This lesson will cover verses 1 and 2, leaving the rest for the next chapter. Within these two verses, there are seven characteristics required of a man who wants to serve as a leader.

His Personal Life

Paul began with a few words for those thinking about serving as leaders.

> It is a trustworthy statement: if any man aspires to the office of overseer, it is a fine work he desires to do. (v. 1)

What exactly is an "overseer"? Commentator Philip H. Towner explains.

> The term translated *overseer* . . . was first used outside the church to refer to supervisors of various sorts. As a description of one level of church leadership, it appears in Acts 20:28 and, again alongside "deacons," in Philippians 1:1. To judge from the account in Paul's farewell meeting with the elders (presbyters; compare 1 Tim. 5:17) of Ephesus (Acts 20:17–38) and the instructions in Titus 1:6–7, the terms "overseer" and "elder" referred to the same office. . . . Among the duties assigned to this office (though

perhaps not exclusively) were preaching and teaching and generally leading or managing the church.[1]

Quite a responsibility! Clearly, aspiration isn't enough for a job of this magnitude. Qualifications must be met:

> An overseer, then, must be above reproach, the husband of one wife, temperate, prudent, respectable, hospitable, able to teach . . . (v. 2)

Let's look at each of these qualifications one by one.

First, an overseer must be *above reproach*. This sounds like a tall order! But the implication is not perfection. Instead, it means he

> must have no flaw in his conduct that would be grounds for any kind of accusation. He must be blameless. . . . A leader within the church should have a good reputation among believers.[2]

Second, a good reputation includes being *the husband of one wife*. The text literally reads "one wife's husband." This requirement presents an interpretive challenge. Does it mean that an overseer must be married, or can he be single? If a man's wife dies and he remarries, is he disqualified? How does divorce affect his credentials? Is this a prohibition against polygamy? Duane Litfin explains:

> The question is, how stringent a standard was Paul erecting for overseers? Virtually all commentators agree that this phrase prohibits both polygamy and promiscuity, which are unthinkable for spiritual leaders in the church. Many Bible students say the words a "one-woman man" are saying that the affections of an elder must be centered exclusively on his wife. Many others hold, however, that the phrase further prohibits any who have been divorced and remarried from becoming overseers. The reasoning behind this view is usually that divorce represents a failure in the home, so that even though a man

---

1 Philip H. Towner, *1–2 Timothy and Titus* (Downers Grove, Ill.: InterVarsity Press, 1994), pp. 82–83.

2 Bruce B. Barton, David R. Veerman, and Neil Wilson, *1 Timothy, 2 Timothy, Titus*, Life Application Bible Commentary Series (Wheaton, Ill.: Tyndale House Publishers, 1993), p. 58.

may be forgiven for any sin involved, he remains permanently disqualified for leadership in the congregation (cf. vv. 4–5; 1 Cor. 9:24–27).[3]

Regarding the specific interpretation of this passage, there are many possibilities. It seems safest, however, to select men who have never been divorced. These men may be widowers who have remarried or men who are currently married with healthy relationships with their wives. Whatever view we adopt, though, one fact remains—an overseer

> must be a man of unquestioned morality, one who is entirely true and faithful to his one and only wife; one who, being married, does not in pagan fashion enter into an immoral relationship with another woman.[4]

Before we appoint leaders, we need to make sure that they exemplify moral purity.

Third, an overseer should also be *temperate*. Paul had in mind here the "self-control necessary for effective ministry" (see also 3:11; Titus 2:2).[5] The Greek term, *nēphalios*, includes having "clarity of mind" and "soberness." Its root word, *nēphō*, means "the opposite of every kind of fuzziness. Sober judgment is highly valued in both individual and public life."[6] A church leader needs to be free from emotional extremism—balanced, not rash.

Fourth, an overseer must be *prudent* (1 Tim. 3:2). The Greek word is *sōphrōn*. It literally means, "of sound mind; self-controlled," which suggests wisdom and discretion.

Wisdom is more than the accumulation of biblical knowledge. It's the application of knowledge to the practicalities of life. It means exercising balanced judgment, avoiding both legalism and moral laxity. It also means having a firm grasp on the real world and the ability to draw on both the Word and personal experience to make decisions.

3. A. Duane Litfin, "1 Timothy," *The Bible Knowledge Commentary*, New Testament edition, ed. John F. Walvoord and Roy B. Zuck (Wheaton, Ill.: Scripture Press Publications, Victor Books, 1983), p. 736.

4. William Hedricksen, *Thessalonians, Timothy, and Titus* (Grand Rapids, Mich.: Baker Book House, 1979), p. 121.

5. *The New International Dictionary of New Testament Theology*, ed. Colin Brown (Grand Rapids, Mich.: Zondervan Publishing House, Regency Reference Library, 1986), vol. 1, p. 515.

6. Gerhard Kittel and Gerhard Friedrich, eds., *Theological Dictionary of the New Testament*, translated and abridged in one volume by Geoffrey W. Bromiley (1985; reprint, Grand Rapids, Mich.: William B. Eerdmans Publishing Co., 1992), p. 634.

Fifth, an overseer must be *respectable*. This word has implications of one who is well-mannered, who behaves in an honorable way.[7] It indicates a man who has gained the respect of those around him and who will continue to earn their respect as he leads.

Sixth, an overseer must be *hospitable*. This requirement may not be readily embraced by those who preach well but can't stand people, but it is a requirement nonetheless. An overseer must not only have an open heart, but an open home as well.

In the days of Paul and Timothy, hospitality was crucial to the survival of the church. At that time, most congregations met in homes, and many still do today, for both teaching and fellowship. Early Christians also took other believers into their homes to rescue them from persecution, provide shelter on a journey, or simply help them survive hardship.

Times and cultures have changed, but the church still needs hospitality. We're a family. We need to open our doors and hearts to the joys, sorrows, and celebrations of others. Sometimes a struggling family needs shelter, or a pregnant teenager needs help. Others may just need encouragement. It's not solely the job of church leaders to provide hospitality, but it is their role to lead the congregation in this responsibility.

Finally, an overseer must be *able to teach*. Does this mean that every leader should be an up-front type or someone who can launch into an hour-long sermon at a moment's notice? Not at all. Rather, this phrase

> speaks of a leader's ability to handle the Scriptures. He must be able both to understand and communicate the truth to others, as well as to refute those who mishandle it (cf. Titus 1:9). Not all must necessarily do this publicly, of course; some may conduct this aspect of their ministries informally in private settings. Yet all leaders must possess an aptitude for handling the Word with skill.[8]

The Scriptures are central to ministry, as Paul said elsewhere in this same letter (1:3–11; 4:6, 11; 6:3–5). It's only natural, then, that ministry leaders should be skilled in handling them.

---

7. Kittel and Friedrich, eds., *Theological Dictionary of the New Testament*, trans. Bromiley, p. 464.

8. A. Duane Litfin, *The Bible Knowledge Commentary*, p. 737.

Do these seven criteria seem daunting, especially since they cover only the first two verses of this passage? The standard is high; there's no doubt about that. But it is not impossible. In fact, many of these criteria represent a standard for all Christians to strive for. And with the Holy Spirit's help, it's within reach.

 Living Insights

It's good that we have God's leadership list to go by. Otherwise, we would tend to choose people with the most impressive credentials or the most pleasing personalities. Though background and disposition are important, God is not impressed with the words on our résumés. He wants to know what is written on our hearts. He's looking for men of character.

Why do you suppose God has such high standards for leadership in His church?

_____

_____

_____

_____

_____

What do the standards in 1 Timothy 3 tell you about:
God's love for His church?

_____

_____

God's desire for His church's holiness?

_____

_____

The importance of knowing people in your congregation?

_____

_____

The accountability of leadership?

_____

_____

The level of spiritual maturity in many churches today?

_____

_____

Chapter 4

A Second Look at First Priorities

1 Timothy 3:3–7

In the previous chapter, we began looking at the list of requirements for church leadership found in 1 Timothy. While it is a helpful tool for evaluating potential candidates, it also tells us about God.

It shows us, for instance, that God knows what characteristics He wants for leaders: He's direct about righteousness, integrity, and faithfulness. You'll find no hazy generalities in this passage. And in this "anything goes" world, isn't it encouraging to know that we serve a God Whose standards don't shift in the winds of relativity and public opinion? (See also Titus 1:5–9; 1 Pet. 5:1–4.)

Notice, too, that Paul's list contains no reference to spiritual gifts. This shows us that God is more interested in leaders who evidence character than those who elevate spiritual gifts. As one Old Testament passage says,

> For the eyes of the Lord move to and fro throughout the earth that He may strongly support those whose heart is completely His. (2 Chron. 16:9a)

God wants leaders whose hearts are set on Him, men who will do whatever it takes to represent righteousness. How can those men be recognized? Let's read on to find out.

Qualifications for Church Leadership

In our last chapter, we looked at seven qualities we should find in the personal life of a qualified overseer. We didn't complete that list, however; 1 Timothy 3:3 offers a few more.

His Personal Life

An overseer, Paul said, should not be

. . . addicted to wine or pugnacious, but gentle,

Parts of this chapter are adapted from "Another Look at the Checklist" in the Bible study guide *Excellence in Ministry: A Study of 1 Timothy*, written by Gary Matlack, from the Bible-teaching ministry of Charles R. Swindoll (Anaheim, Calif.: Insight for Living, 1996).

peaceable, free from the love of money. (v. 3)

First, *a church leader should not be "addicted to wine."* In Greek, there is a single word that covers this phrase: *paroinos*. The parts of the word, *para*, "beside," and *oinos*, "wine," describe a person who spends too much time "beside the wine"—in other words, under the control of alcohol.

Why is this a matter for concern? Because overdrinking can cloud the mind and blunt the senses—conditions that hinder good leadership. For how can a man shepherd a flock if he becomes mentally or emotionally unstable? And who can follow or respect such an incapacitated leader?

Another problem overdrinking suggests is that a man has some underlying need he is avoiding rather than trying to face. He is numbing himself to reality (compare Ps. 51:6a). How, then, can a man lead others into truth when he's running from it himself? If he doesn't resolve his inner turmoil, his drinking will destroy his life and slowly poison the church.

Drunkenness violates God's standard, not just for leaders but for all Christians (read Rom. 13:12–14; 1 Cor. 5:11; Gal. 5:19–21; Eph. 5:18; 1 Pet. 4:1–5). God wants us to be clear-thinking, alert, discerning individuals who are capable of making sound decisions.

Second, *a church leader should not be pugnacious.* Now there's an old-fashioned word for you! The Greek phrase for "not pugnacious" literally means "not a striker."[1] Paul was warning us away from someone who's quick with the blows, always looking for a fight, be it physical or verbal.

Someone who consistently responds to criticism with defensiveness or anger is not in a position to take on a church leadership role. We are all in the process of maturing, but this is one area elders and pastors need to have mastered. Like Jesus, church leaders need to have learned to hand judgment and retribution over to the Father (see 1 Pet. 2:21–23).

Does this mean that a leader can't ever get angry or that he should make pleasing people his priority? No. But a good leader knows how to take the heat without spreading the flames.

Third, *a church leader should be gentle.* The Greek word for gentle, *epieikes*, can also be translated "yielding" or "forbearing." Someone

---

1. William Hendricksen, *Thessalonians, Timothy and Titus,* New Testament Commentary Series (Grand Rapids, Mich.: Baker Book House, 1979), p. 125.

once said this meant to pardon human failings; to look to the law-giver, not to the law; to the intention, not to the action; to the whole, not to the part; to the character of the actor in the long run and not in the present moment; to remember good rather than evil, and the good that one has received rather than the good that one has done; to bear being injured; to wish to settle a matter by words rather than deeds.

And as William Barclay has said,

> If there is a matter under dispute, it can be settled by consulting a book of practice and procedure, or it can be settled by consulting Jesus Christ. If there is a matter of debate, it can be settled in law, or it can be settled in love.[2]

That philosophy is the essence of gentleness.

Fourth, *a church leader should be peaceable*. The New International Version of this passage translates the Greek term as "not quarrelsome." Philip H. Towner explains that a quarrelsome person

> betrays an inability to get along with and accept the views of others, and perhaps deeper personality flaws as well. The false teachers in Ephesus were known for their quarrels (1:5; 6:4–5). A leader prone to this weakness will produce discord instead of harmony. But a leader, or any Christian for that matter, who promotes peace among people will create and preserve the relationships necessary for building a unified church.[3]

Some leaders are, as Barclay puts it, "trigger-happy" in their relationships.[4] Quick on the draw, itching for a good argument. But a godly leader keeps his gun holstered until he needs it for the real enemy. He listens to others. He cooperates. He builds people up instead of tearing them down.

---

2. William Barclay, *The Letters to Timothy, Titus, and Philemon*, rev. ed., The Daily Study Bible Series (Philadelphia, Pa.: Westminster Press, 1975), pp. 83–84.

3. Philip H. Towner, *1–2 Timothy and Titus*, The IVP New Testament Commentary Series (Downers Grove, Ill.: InterVarsity Press, 1994), p. 87.

4. Barclay, *The Letters to Timothy, Titus, and Philemon*, p. 84.

Fifth, *a church leader should be free from the love of money*. For too many people today, blessing and success are measured in dollars and cents. How misleading! Yet money itself is not the problem. As author Gene Getz pointed out, it's our attitude toward it that gets us into trouble.

> The Scriptures do not teach that "money" per se is evil. Nor do they teach that it is wrong to have lots of money. What they do teach is that it is a serious violation of God's will when we *love it*. That is why Paul said that a mature Christian man is "free," not from money, but "from the love of money."[5]

Our attitude toward material wealth, Towner explains,

> ought to be one of healthy detachment, but certainly not irresponsibility. Such a leader can be a model of generosity and simplicity of lifestyle because of the knowledge that whatever one's economic status might be, all that one has belongs to God and so must be looked after faithfully before him (6:17–19).[6]

A godly leader loves God and uses money, not the other way around. (See also Matt. 6:24; Titus 1:7; 1 Pet. 5:2.)

His Domestic Life: A Good Household Manager

Having covered the personal characteristics of a qualified church leader, Paul moves on to describe his domestic life.

> He must be one who manages his own household well, keeping his children under control with all dignity (but if a man does not know how to manage his own household, how will he take care of the church of God?). (1 Tim. 3:4–5)

It is significant that Paul's only reference to management in this passage concerned the home, not the business world. Leading the church certainly involves management—of time, priorities, staff, programs, and more—but Paul's focus was on the home and family.

---

5. Gene A. Getz, *The Measure of a Man* (Ventura, Calif.: Gospel Light Publications, Regal Books, 1995), p. 193.

6. Towner, *1–2 Timothy and Titus*, p. 87.

Why? Because the church is a family, not a business. It has a heavenly Father, not a CEO. Brothers and sisters, not shareholders. We have a Groom, Jesus Christ, not an impersonal boss.

Here's the straight scoop. It doesn't matter if a man succeeds at everything else in life; if he's not leading his family well, he's disqualified from leading the church. Far too many men are up to their kneecaps in business, church work, and other endeavors—and often enjoying success in all these areas. But their homes are in disarray. If you want to know how a man is going to lead the church, look at his home life.

A word of caution, though: nobody's home is going to be perfect twenty-four hours a day. Even the preacher's kid is going to run wild down the aisle of the grocery store now and then. So, what we need to look for is the general tenor of the home. Are the kids usually respectful and the home basically well-ordered? Are the parents attentive, involved, and supportive of each other and their children? How is the communication? Is an atmosphere of spiritual development being fostered? Is Jesus Christ openly discussed and revered? Is the Word studied?

A man who has these priorities for his family possesses the qualities of a leader worth following.

His Spiritual Life: Not a New Convert

Next, Paul discussed the spiritual life of a church leader. He said this man should be

> not a new convert, so that he will not become conceited and fall into the condemnation incurred by the devil. (v. 6)

The role of an elder calls for roots. It calls for perception, experience, and wisdom. It calls for someone who has been seasoned by life's triumphs, failures, joys, and disappointments.

A brand-new believer, right out of the spiritual womb, may have enthusiasm. He may have learned a lot about the Bible in a short span of time. He may have turned his life around and begun to exhibit many godly traits—but he can also easily fall victim to discouragement or, on the other hand, pride. Only the growing pains of maturity produce stability and a humble heart.

His Public Life: A Good Reputation

With all these things in place, the next thing to examine is the man's public life.

> And he must have a good reputation with those outside the church, so that he will not fall into reproach and the snare of the devil. (v. 7)

Are you surprised to find this qualification on the list? After all, what does the surrounding community have to do with choosing leaders in the church? Well, the world observes the candidate's lifestyle too. And remember, reputation matters.

Is this man friendly? How does he handle conflict? Disagreement? How did he respond when the neighbor's kid knocked a ball through the living room window? How does he treat the dry cleaner, the grocery checker, and the waitress? We can often discover a lot about a man from the neighbors who have nothing to gain or lose from his appointment to leadership.

It's important, though, to understand that some people dislike Christians simply because they're Christians. So feedback from neighbors must, as should all input, be received with discretion.

A Few Questions regarding Potential Leaders

Well, that's Paul's profile for elders. Let's wrap up our discussion with three questions we should ask of those who want to serve in any facet of church leadership.

Personally, do his internals square with his externals? He speaks well in public. He's well-mannered and neat. He handles himself well under pressure. But does his inner character measure up to his outward appearance?

Domestically, would his family vote for him? How would a candidate's wife and kids respond? Would they agree that he "manages his own household well"? Or does the home function in spite of him?

Publicly, will the community be surprised or affirming? Would people in his workplace nod and smile at the news of his nomination? Or would they look puzzled and ask, "Wait a minute. Are we talking about the same guy?"

Extensive qualifications? Yes. Unreasonable? No. God takes leadership seriously. The Good Shepherd loves His sheep too much to leave us unprotected. And men with character are the best defense against wolves.

Living Insights

Paul's list provides an important principle for these days, when so many church leaders are spiraling down to ruin like sputtering, smoking planes: leading begins with following. Following God, that is. Each of the qualities on Paul's list—moral purity, hospitality, gentleness, sobriety, and so on—sprout from a nourishing, obedient relationship with Jesus Christ. His Spirit produces these qualities in our lives as we follow Him.

Jonathan Edwards wrote:

> [Ministers] should earnestly seek after much of the spiritual knowledge of Christ, and that they may live in clear views of his glory. For by this means they will be changed into the image of the same glory and brightness, and will come to their people, as Moses came down to the congregation of Israel . . . with his face shining. If the light of Christ's glory shines upon them, it will be the way for them to shine with the same kind of light on their hearers, and to reflect the same beams, which have heat, as well as brightness. . . . Ministers should be much in seeking God, and conversing with Him by prayer, who is the fountain of light and love.[7]

Are you a leader? If so, are you spending adequate time with Christ, enriching your soul so you can enrich others? If you need to, what adjustments can you make in your schedule to allow for this?

_____

_____

_____

_____

_____

_____

7. Iain H. Murray, *Jonathan Edwards: A New Biography* (1987; reprint, Carlisle, Pa.: Banner of Truth Trust, 1992), p. 144.

What about other leaders in your church? How can you encourage them or help free them up to spend more time in God's presence?

_____

_____

_____

_____

_____

The power for ministry doesn't rest in programs; it rests in a Person. So let's lead, first of all, by following Him.

Chapter 5

TWO DIFFERENT
STYLES OF CHURCHES

Acts 2:41, 47; 4:4; 6:1–4; Exodus 18:7–24

When it comes to churches, why is *big* often considered *bad*?

Think about it. Don't we sometimes give big churches a bum rap? We look at their large staffs and wonder, "What do all of those paid people do all day?" We see their budget figures and question, "Where does all that money go?" Or we wonder how so many people could possibly be ministered to in any kind of personal way.

Yes, *big* is often a bad word when it comes to churches. Yet we consider bigger to be better in other settings. By and large, we'd rather shop in a big mall than a small one. We'd prefer to be sick in a large hospital, buy stock in a large company, hire an employee from a large university. But when it comes to big churches . . . well, we have our doubts.

Why is that, do you suppose? Is it just a preference thing? Or do small churches more closely follow the model of New Testament congregations? Just what were those early churches like, anyway? Let's look back in history and find out.

The First Church

When Christ ascended to heaven, He left behind a small group of believers to carry out the Great Commission—His command to take the gospel to the world. This left-behind group was initially a fellowship of about 120 people, mostly made up of the disciples and their families, along with a few others (Acts 1:15). But then came Pentecost. At this momentous event, the Holy Spirit indwelled the disciples and enabled them to speak in various languages, allowing them to proclaim the gospel to everyone who had gathered in Jerusalem. When some onlookers accused the disciples of being

Parts of this chapter are adapted from "The Difference Between a Metropolitan Church and a Neighborhood Church" in the Bible study guide *The Bride*, written by Gary Matlack, from the Bible-teaching ministry of Charles R. Swindoll (Anaheim, Calif.: Insight for Living, 1994).

drunk, Peter stood up and delivered a powerful sermon, a message that would change the church forever.

It Had Size and Growth

Acts 2:41 records the response to Peter's sermon:

> So then, those who had received his word were baptized; and that day there were added about three thousand souls.

Up to this point, the small group of believers had been able to meet in a single home, in the "upper room" (Acts 1:13).[1] But not anymore! The addition of three thousand members turned them into an instant megachurch. And the growth didn't stop there.

> And the Lord was adding to their number day by day those who were being saved. (2:47b)

The group was now a truly big church and was getting bigger by the day. But was it just a fad? A one-sermon wonder, a shooting star destined to die out as quickly and boldly as it had appeared? Time would soon tell, for just as the church was attracting excitement, it also was drawing the scorn of Jerusalem's Jewish leaders. The Sadducees came to Peter's second sermon armed with the captain of the temple guard and had Peter and John thrown in jail (4:1–3). But did this persecution stunt the church's growth? Not at all.

> But many of those who had heard the message believed; and the number of the men came to be about five thousand. (4:4)

Notice that it was only the men who numbered 5,000. Sometimes the New Testament uses the term *anthropos*, often rendered "men," to describe a mixed group containing both men and women. The Greek term used in verse 4, however, is *aner*, which describes only males. This means that the total church membership, including women and children, could have numbered at least twice that amount!

The image of the first church as a small, neighborhood congregation just doesn't fit with the reality, at least not after Pentecost. After that, it became a full-scale metropolitan operation.

---

1. Two-story houses were not uncommon in Palestine during the New Testament period. Families often lived on the second floor, using the bottom floor for storage. The "upper room" used by the fledgling church must have been a large guest room able to accommodate its 100-plus members.

It Wasn't Perfect

The new church was really moving and growing. They were doing a lot of things well—teaching, worshiping, evangelizing, and sharing (Acts 2:42–46). But they were not perfect. Like any church facing rapid growth, they faced some challenges along the way.

> Now at this time while the disciples were in-creasing in number, a complaint arose on the part of the Hellenistic Jews against the native Hebrews, because their widows were being overlooked in the daily serving of food. (6:1)

Two groups made up the Jerusalem church, the *Hellēnistai* (Greek Jews) and the *Hebraioi* (Hebrew Jews).[2] The *Hellēnistai* came from the diaspora; they had settled in Palestine and spoke Greek. The *Hebraioi*, on the other hand, were natives of Palestine and spoke Aramaic. The distinction between the two groups, however, went beyond origin and language, as John Stott notes:

> In this case the *Hellēnistai* not only spoke Greek but thought and behaved like Greeks, while the *Hebraioi* not only spoke Aramaic but were deeply immersed in Hebrew culture. . . . There had always, of course, been rivalry between these groups in Jewish culture; the tragedy is that it was perpetuated within the new community of Jesus who by his death had abolished such distinctions.[3]

Despite what they had in common—new life in Christ—the two groups were still having trouble getting along. The tensions reached a boiling point over an issue most people cared little about: the feeding of widows. But when the Greek Jews realized that their widows were receiving less favorable treatment than the Hebrews' widows, they saw it as a slight upon all of the *Hellēnistai*. And they made a public case out of it, bringing it to the disciples' attention.

The disciples were appropriately concerned. Yet they were torn: the matter needed to be dealt with, but taking care of it would distract them from their primary responsibility—that of teaching

---

2. John R. W. Stott, *The Spirit, the Church, and the World: The Message of Acts* (Downers Grove, Ill.: InterVarsity Press, 1990), p. 120.

3. Stott, *The Spirit, the Church, and the World*, pp. 120–121.

the Word. So they delegated the task to "men of good reputation, full of the Spirit and of wisdom" (v. 3). And a positive solution was found for a potentially detrimental situation.

A Lesson from the Life of Moses

Perhaps the disciples so quickly delegated authority—often a hard thing to do—because they had heard the story of Moses, who faced a similar situation.

Moses' Bad Situation

Moses had no ministry experience; he'd been herding sheep in the desert for forty years. Then suddenly, at the ripe age of eighty, he found himself recruited by God to pastor "Wilderness Bible Church," a congregation of about two million cantankerous souls recently released from slavery. And the demands of the ministry engulfed him like a sandstorm, a problem Moses' father-in-law, Jethro, witnessed firsthand.

> It came about the next day that Moses sat to judge the people, and the people stood about Moses from the morning until the evening. Now when Moses' father-in-law saw all that he was doing for the people, he said, "What is this thing that you are doing for the people? Why do you alone sit as judge and all the people stand about you from morning until evening?" Moses said to his father-in-law, "Because the people come to me to inquire of God. When they have a dispute, it comes to me and I judge between a man and his neighbor and make known the statutes of God and His laws." Moses' father-in-law said to him, "The thing that you are doing is not good. You will surely wear out, both yourself and these people who are with you, for the task is too heavy for you; you cannot do it alone." (Exod. 18:13–18)

Moses was trapped on a treadmill of a one-man ministry. Driven by the desire to blend God's Law into the life of every Israelite, he was in danger of wearing out. The people were headed for exhaustion too. Can you imagine waiting in line all day to see Moses and have your problems ironed out?

Jethro's Good Advice

Thankfully, Jethro followed up his questions with an answer.

> "Now listen to me: I will give you counsel, and God be with you. You be the people's representative before God, and you bring the disputes to God, then teach them the statutes and the laws, and make known to them the way in which they are to walk and the work they are to do. Furthermore, you shall select out of all the people able men who fear God, men of truth, those who hate dishonest gain; and you shall place these over them as leaders of thousands, of hundreds, of fifties and of tens. Let them judge the people at all times; and let it be that every major dispute they will bring to you, but every minor dispute they themselves will judge. So it will be easier for you, and they will bear the burden with you. If you do this thing and God so commands you, then you will be able to endure, and all these people also will go to their place in peace." (vv. 19–23)

Two key lessons emerge from Jethro's counsel. First, he stressed *communication*. Look again at verse 20: "Teach them the statutes and the laws." Is it merely a coincidence that the apostles kept the same priority in Acts 6?

Second, Jethro taught *delegation*. "Pass around the workload," he urged, but not just to any willing warm body. Note the qualifications in verse 21: "Able men who fear God, men of truth, those who hate dishonest gain . . ." Sounds a lot like the men chosen by the apostles to feed the widows, doesn't it?

How do the examples of Moses and the apostles specifically apply to churches today? Whether a congregation has an overworked solo pastor or a large staff flooded with requests, the following facts apply:

1. Many people, plus high expectations, multiplied by numerous needs, equals *endless* responsibilities.

2. As the work of the ministry increases, the load must be shifted—efficiency is sometimes revealed not in what we accomplish, but in what we *relinquish*.

3. God's servants are not exempt from physical limitations. Too

much work and not enough rest can make anyone ill, anxious, bitter, or broken.

Two Kinds of Churches

One concern about big churches is that the needs of many people will go unmet. And that would be true if a pastor tried to handle it all on his own. But Moses and the disciples show us that big is not necessarily bad, that growth and size need not be negatives if they are handled appropriately. The disciples could have simply split the church into two or more smaller, more manageable ones. Moses and Jethro could have directed each of the twelve tribes to form their own autonomous states. And there may have been nothing wrong with those solutions. But by finding other ways to manage the masses, these godly leaders proved that a big body of believers can also be a good one.

We're all different. Some of us like the opportunities and excitement of a large congregation; others feel lost in a crowd and prefer a smaller, more intimate fellowship. It's easy to point out the advantages or disadvantages of either one . . . but instead, let's accept and even celebrate the fact that churches of all sizes can find God's favor.

It's important to note, though, that churches of different sizes operate and think differently. The mentality of a small, neighborhood church differs greatly from that of a large, metropolitan one. If you're looking for a church, maybe the following chart will help you determine whether a large one or a small one might fit you best.

The "Neighborhood" Concept	The "Metropolitan" Concept
Close ties between the pastor and people: a feeling of being one family who identifies with the pastor	Close ties between identity groups: a feeling of being among numerous families who identify with one another
Smaller scale regarding: staff, vision, organization, facilities, budget, outreach, variety	Larger scale regarding: staff, vision, organization, facilities, budget, outreach, variety
Congregation mainly from a close radius in the community	Congregation drawn from a vast radius
Tendency to be "inbred": narrow rotation among lay leadership, possibly greater resistance to change	Less "inbred": broad rotation among lay leadership, less resistance to change

The "Neighborhood" Concept	The "Metropolitan" Concept
Easy to know everyone	Impossible to know everyone
Workload borne by volunteers	Some work delegated to specialists
Relatively simple to manage and maintain	Complex to manage and maintain
Usually a one-man operation, so the pastor's personality may set the tone for the church's atmosphere	Large staff, causing a broader base of control
Strong, centralized loyalty to the church, which makes it easier to implement involvement	Loyalty decentralized to various ministries, more difficult to implement improvement
A naturally warm and friendly atmosphere	Atmosphere can still be warm and friendly, but an ongoing challenge to maintain

Keep These Things in Mind

As you contemplate the differences between a metropolitan and a neighborhood church mentality, keep these practical suggestions in mind:

- *God determines which church is which.* God determined the sizes of Moses' and the apostles' congregations. He still decides today.

- *You determine which size and mentality fits your own gifts and needs.* When it comes to choosing a church, assess your desires and needs. No matter what anyone else likes, you need to decide for yourself what kind of church is the best fit for you.

- *You must accept and adapt if you decide to stay at a church.* Since a church cannot change its size or mentality unless God calls it to do so, you must accept a church for what it is and adapt to it if you decide to make it your home.

- *No matter how big or small a church is, it must never ignore problems or omit priorities.* Some things hold true regardless of size. Solving problems and maintaining priorities are two things all churches must do.

Living Insights

Regardless of the size of church you attend now, what kind of church would be the best fit for you? Go back to the chart that compares the neighborhood church with the metropolitan church.

1. What things about a neighborhood church appeal to you? What things about a neighborhood church strike you as drawbacks?

_____

_____

_____

_____

2. What things about a metropolitan church appeal to you? What things about a metropolitan church strike you as drawbacks?

_____

_____

_____

_____

3. What things about a neighborhood church would be advantageous for your family at this time? What things about a neighborhood church might be detrimental for your family right now?

_____

_____

_____

_____

4. What things about a metropolitan church would be advantageous for your family at this time? What things about a metropolitan church might be detrimental for your family right now?

_____

_____

_____

_____

5. Overall, which model seems to fit you and your family best?

_____

_____

_____

_____

Before making any decisions, go to God in prayer. Ask Him if you should stay where you are and adapt, or if you should make a change. And remember, God promises to give wisdom to those who ask Him for it (James 1:5).

Chapter 6

KEEPING THE CHURCH
BALANCED IN TRENDY TIMES
Selected Scriptures

Yยou've heard of the television show, *Battle of the Sexes*. Let's take a minute to conduct our own contest, a short *Battle of the Generations*, by asking people of different ages to answer this seemingly simple question: When were the "good old days"?

Pearl, a 75-year-old grandmother of twelve, steps to the microphone first. "That's easy," she opens. "The good old days came in the 1940s, when the big bands played and six decades of the industrial revolution made life easier than ever."

The next contestant quickly disagrees. Bob, 61, claims, "The best times were clearly the fifties—sock hops and hot rods ruled. You can't get any better than that! And we certainly didn't have any Hitlers walking around."

Pearl's daughter, Janet, 52, argues for the sixties. "Who needs Hitler when you've got your own people hurting each other— whites oppressing blacks, men suppressing women, and everyone ignoring Native Americans who were practically dying from their own poverty. For the first time in history, during the sixties, the nation's young people made their voices heard. We spoke our minds and embraced high ideals. We made a difference."

Her younger brother, Billy, offers still another opinion. "I know everybody gets down on the 70s, but man, they were cool." Pearl rolls her eyes, Bob snickers, and Janet mumbles something sarcastic, under her breath, about disco music and powder-blue, polyester leisure suits.

Dreaming about the "good old days" can be fun, or at least funny. But as we've seen, not everyone agrees about *when* they actually took place.

Here's another volatile question—when did the "good old days" occur for the church? On second thought, let's not consider that question. It's probably best left unanswered. Why? Because reminiscing, as fun as it is, can be dangerous for the church. It can distract us from our current mission—to reach today's world for Christ. That's not to say that we as individuals can't or shouldn't muse about our own "good old days," but the church—as a whole—can't afford to spend any time idolizing the past. We certainly can't use the "good old days" as an excuse to shun or disconnect from the present. After all, it takes practically all our energy just to stay relevant to society, to keep fully engaged with it at all times.

Yet there's another side of church life that we must also consider—we're commanded to stay rooted in God's timeless Word. We're prohibited from becoming like the world in which we live. We must resist its temptations, refusing to think like it or be like it in any significant way.

This apparent contradiction creates for us a unique struggle—we need to minister to our world without becoming part of it. We have to stay current with our culture while remaining true to our ancient faith. We need to be relevant, yet biblical. In other words, we need to stay *balanced*.

How can we achieve this kind of balance? God's Word offers several examples to help us formulate an answer.

Examples of Balance from the Bible

The balancing act we face today is nothing new. The problem, in fact, existed way back in the days of the Old Testament. The Hebrew Scriptures report several success stories of people who struggled to maintain their balance and won.

Daniel

Most people know Daniel from his night in the lions' den and his prophecies of the last days. Far fewer know about his younger years. He grew up in Palestine, but when he was just a teenager, King Nebuchadnezzar besieged Judah and took everyone to Babylon (Dan. 1:1–2). From the captives, the king selected the best youths, including Daniel, to be trained for his service. The king taught them according to the highest Chaldean standards and even offered them the best foods from his own supply (vv. 3–5).

Although the king's food was the best money could buy, it violated the Hebrews' strict dietary laws. Most of the young people apparently ate the food to avoid offending the king. Daniel, however, refused.

> But Daniel made up his mind that he would not defile himself with the king's choice food or with the wine which he drank; so he sought permission

from the commander of the officials that he might
not defile himself. (v. 8)

God blessed Daniel's stand. The Lord moved in the heart of
the commander, compelling him to grant Daniel's request (v. 14),
and supplied Daniel with so much nourishment that he actually
looked better than the youths who ate the king's food (v. 15). As
a result, Daniel was allowed to continue eating according to the
laws of his faith.

But Daniel didn't shun Babylonian society altogether. He learned
their ways, their literature, and wisdom (v. 17). He even became
one of the king's most trusted consultants and dream interpreters
(vv. 19–20). During one interpretation, Daniel gave glory and
credit to the One who had protected him and allowed him to thrive
in his pagan surroundings:

> Daniel said,
> "Let the name of God be blessed forever and ever,
> For wisdom and power belong to Him.
> "It is He who changes the times and the epochs;
> He removes kings and establishes kings;
> He gives wisdom to wise men
> And knowledge to men of understanding.
> "It is He who reveals the profound and hidden
>   things;
> He knows what is in the darkness,
> And the light dwells with Him.
> "To You, O God of my fathers, I give thanks and
>   praise,
> For You have given me wisdom and power;
> Even now You have made known to me what we
>   requested of You,
> For you have made known to us the king's
>   matter." (2:20–23)

Daniel kept his life in balance—he clung to his faith, but also
adapted to his new surroundings. And throughout his days, he
stayed true to God and believed that the Lord would protect him
when his faith collided with his culture. That same faith in God
can keep us balanced too, if we'll truly trust in Him.

David

David, too, had to walk the balance beam, which at times probably seemed more like a death plank. Like Daniel, his faith clashed with his culture more than once.

> Be gracious to me, O Lord, for I am in
>   distress. . . .
> Because of all my adversaries, I have become a
>   reproach,
> Especially to my neighbors,
> And an object of dread to my acquaintances;
> Those who see me in the street flee from me.
> I am forgotten as a dead man, out of mind;
> I am like a broken vessel.
> For I have heard the slander of many,
> Terror is on every side;
> While they took counsel together against me,
> They schemed to take away my life.
> (Ps. 31:9a, 11–13)

What a way to live! But David's faith, like Daniel's, protected and sustained him through the difficult times.

> But as for me, I trust in you, O Lord,
> I say, "You are my God."
> My times are in Your hand;
> Deliver me from the hand of my enemies and
>   from those who persecute me.
> Make Your face to shine upon Your servant;
> Save me in Your lovingkindness.
> Let me not be put to shame, O Lord, for I call
>   upon You;
> Let the wicked be put to shame, let them be
>   silent in Sheol.
> Let the lying lips be mute,
> Which speak arrogantly against the righteous
> With pride and contempt. (vv. 14–18)

What faith! David truly believed that God would protect him, despite the attempts by many to take his life.

When our culture tries to press us into its mold and persecutes us for resisting, it's tempting to go to extremes—either to give in and become like the world or to pull up our stakes and leave, isolating ourselves in a Christian bubble. Neither option pleases God, Who wants us to stay balanced. For the sake of the gospel, we need to stay engaged, yet remain unwavering in our standards. Only through David-like faith can we muster the courage to do both and the strength to endure the scorn that will come as a result.

Paul

Balancing acts aren't exclusive to the Old Testament side of the Scriptures. Saints in the New Testament had to do their share of balancing as well—Paul most of all. And his teachings reflect his experience. On the one hand, he commanded his Roman readers:

> Do not be conformed to this world, but be transformed by the renewing of your mind, so that you may prove what the will of God is, that which is good and acceptable and perfect. (Romans 12:2)

Yet on the other hand, just a few verses later, he exhorted them:

> Every person is to be in subjection to the governing authorities. For there is no authority except from God, and those which exist are established by God. Therefore whoever resists authority has opposed the ordinance of God; and they who have opposed will receive condemnation upon themselves. (13:1–2)

Paul knew the importance of balance. He experienced the need for it in his own life, and he passed his knowledge on to his contemporaries. But Paul knew that balance was a requirement not limited to believers in his own day. He understood that balance would become even harder to maintain in the future:

> But realize this, that in the last days difficult times will come. For men will be lovers of self, lovers of money, boastful, arrogant, revilers, disobedient to parents, ungrateful, unholy, unloving, irreconcilable, malicious gossips, without self-control, brutal, haters of good, treacherous, reckless, conceited, lovers of pleasure rather than lovers of God, holding to a form of godliness, although they have denied its power; Avoid such men as these. . . . You, however, continue in the things you have learned and become

convinced of, knowing from whom you have learned
them. (2 Tim. 3:1–5, 14)

Doesn't this description seem to fit our world today? More and
more, it seems like we're getting close to the last days. And balance
is becoming more and more difficult to maintain. The farther from
godly values the world strays, the more we have to stretch to stay
relevant to our culture yet true to God's Word. It's a difficult task,
but not an impossible one.

Requirements for Keeping Balance

To keep our balance in these increasingly difficult times, we
must realize one thing: *we must be willing to leave the familiar without
disturbing the essentials*. We need to do away with outdated methods,
but preserve our core values. Here are two suggestions for maintaining that delicate balance.

Use Discernment

Changing times require that churches be willing to retool and
flex where needed. We need to keep evaluating and rethinking our
approach to ministry. Do we need to update our style of worship
by adding in some fresh and creative music alongside the traditional
hymns? Do we need to bring technology to the pulpit to support
our pastors' sermons with computer-generated presentations? How
can we use the Internet to spread the gospel message?

Conversely, how can we continue to minister to those who have
grown up in the church, who love the old traditions and feel left
out of the changes? And how can we update our methods without
compromising our message? Finding wise answers to these questions
requires discernment, and discernment comes through paying attention, asking insightful questions, and proceeding with prayer.

Hang on to Discipline

Discernment helps us know what to do, but we need discipline
to carry it out. Discernment shows us where to change; discipline
keeps us from changing too much. God's truths, for example, are timeless; they require no adaptation, though the world would like to
take what we offer and tweak it to make it more comfortable. We
need to hold tight to God's Word, but extend it in a manner the
world can relate to. Maintaining the basic spiritual disciplines will
help us keep our balance as we fiddle with our means of expression.

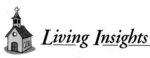

Living Insights

> A charge to keep I have,
> A God to glorify,
> A never-dying soul to save,
> And fit it for the sky.
>
> To serve the present age,
> My calling to fulfill,
> Oh, may it all my pow'rs engage
> To do my Master's will.[1]

Charles Wesley's hymn reveals his awareness of the time in which he lived. He and his brother John ministered in the "present age" of eighteenth-century England, traveling thousands of miles on horseback to preach the Word to people who had no pastor or congregational family. Acutely aware that theology had become too dry and lofty for many lay people, Charles crafted his thoughts not only into sermons, but also into hymns. This was just one of the many creative ways the Wesleys communicated the truths of God's Word to keep them fresh and interesting and relevant for the people of their day.

Are you in touch with our present age? Do you know the issues affecting the church and the world? Are you up with the times, or are you lagging behind in the "good old days"? Don't look now, but some of us are guilty of addressing questions people stopped asking years ago.

The good news is that it's never too late to learn. If you feel out of touch, take some time this week to fix the problem. Read a newspaper to get a feel for where society is; talk to different people—friends and strangers alike—to find out how they feel about church and religion.

Then delve back into the Scriptures, asking God to help you live out His timeless truths in a constantly changing world. In other words, ask Him to help you keep your balance in these trendy times.

This Living Insights section is adapted from "What Changes and What Doesn't" in the Bible study guide *The Bride*, written by Gary Matlack, from the Bible-teaching ministry of Charles R. Swindoll (Anaheim, Calif.: Insight for Living, 1994).

1. Charles Wesley, "A Charge to Keep I Have," in *New Songs of Inspiration* (Dallas, Tex.: Zondervan Corporation, Stamps-Baxter Music, 1982), vol. 8, no. 21.

One new thing I've learned about my world this week is:

_____

_____

_____

_____

_____

I plan to change, in order to be a better witness for God, in light of that fact:

_____

_____

_____

_____

_____

Chapter 7
"AND WHEN YOU PRAY..."
Matthew 6:5–15

Prayer. It's just as important to church life as it is to our private lives. And it's so simple. There's no complicated formula. No rigid schedule. No intricate instructions on recitation or posture. Prayer as God intended it is just conversation—just talking with Him. But, like so many of the simple things of God, we tend to make it more complicated, repackaging it in rigid, religious formulas.

Why? Not because we don't believe in prayer, but precisely because we do—just as the Jews in Jesus' day did. William Barclay tells us that the rabbis used to say,

> "Great is prayer, greater than all good works."[1]

And,

> "He who prays within his house surrounds it with a wall that is stronger than iron." The only regret of the Rabbis was that it was not possible to pray all the day long.[2]

Prayer is wonderful. It connects us with God and keeps us walking in His ways. But the truth is, our church prayer times so often leave us feeling flat, even disconnected from God. Like the Jews, modern-day Christians tend to approach prayer in ways that sometimes undermine its effectiveness.

What Went Wrong with Prayer

The Jews were serious about prayer—and that was as it should have been. But for some, their seriousness turned into an unhealthy intensity. Their expectations became impossibly high, and the many who couldn't live up to them found themselves weighed down by

Parts of this chapter are adapted from "Strengthening Your Grip on Prayer" in the Bible study guide *Strengthening Your Grip*, written by Ken Gire and Gary Matlack, from the Bible-teaching ministry of Charles R. Swindoll (Anaheim, Calif.: Insight for Living, 1995).

1. William Barclay, *The Gospel of Matthew*, vol. 1, rev. ed., The Daily Bible Series (Philadelphia, Pa.: Westminster Press, 1975), p. 191.

2. William Barclay, *The Gospel of Matthew*, p. 191.

guilt rather than comforted by the Spirit. By the time Jesus stepped onto the religious scene, prayer had degenerated in at least four ways.

It Had Become Formal and Ritualistic

There was little room for spontaneity in the Jewish system of prayer. Though some people recited prescribed liturgy with heartfelt devotion, most had fallen into a routine of checking prayer off their "to do" list. The Jews had specific prayers and creeds to recite at certain times. The *Shema*, for example (consisting of Deut. 6:4–9; 11:13–21; and Num. 15:37–41), had to be recited by every Jew, every morning and every evening, before 9 A.M. and before 9 P.M.[3]

In addition, the truly pious prayed three more times daily— 9 A.M., noon, and 3 P.M.—regardless of where they were or what they were doing. And they had to do it in a particular position— arms out, palms up, head bowed. In addition, Barclay explains,

> The Jewish liturgy supplied stated prayers for all occasions. There was hardly an event or a sight in life which had not its stated formula of prayer. There was prayer before and after each meal; there were prayers in connection with the light, the fire, the lightning, on seeing the new moon, comets, rain, tempest, at the sight of the sea, lakes, rivers, on receiving good news, on using new furniture, on entering or leaving a city. Everything had its prayer.[4]

It Had Become Long and Verbose

A rabbi once said, "Whoever is long in prayer is heard."[5] One popular prayer in Jesus' day even had sixteen adjectives in front of God's name! There's nothing wrong with pouring out your heart to the Lord; He loves to hear our voices. But sometimes prayers are long on words and short on substance. The person praying, at times, appears to be more concerned with how he sounds rather than Whom he is addressing. When the focus of the prayer shifts from content to format, the words become empty and the results negligible.

3. William Barclay, *The Gospel of Matthew*, p. 192.

4. William Barclay, *The Gospel of Matthew*, pp. 193–94.

5. William Barclay, *The Gospel of Matthew*, p. 195.

It Had Become Repetitious

Prayer had become "a kind of intoxication with words."[6] Those who strove for piety lost themselves in hypnotic chants. Their emphasis had shifted from the message of prayer to the mechanics of it.

It Had Become Prideful

For the religious leaders of Jesus' day, prayer had become a glass case in which the glittering jewels of piety were displayed. Men were known to stop on the steps of the synagogue at appointed prayer times and dazzle onlookers with their lengthy prayers. They were clearly praying for men, not to God.

As you can imagine, if people didn't conform to the correct style, they weren't considered to be truly devoted to God. Living up to others' expectations became the primary motivation for praying.

What Jesus Taught about Prayer

Into this rigid system of dos and don'ts came Jesus with His own instructions on prayer. Like a pebble in the highly polished shoe of Judaism, He irritated the self-impressed religious leaders—He offered freedom from their chains of legalism by teaching that prayer was made for the ears of God, not the applause of men. In His Sermon on the Mount, He gave three pieces of general advice on prayer, which we can apply to our corporate petitions as well as to our private ones.

Avoid Hypocrisy

> "When you pray, you are not to be like the hypocrites; for they love to stand and pray in the synagogues and on the street corners so that they may be seen by men. Truly I say to you, they have their reward in full. But you, when you pray, go into your inner room, close your door and pray to your Father who is in secret, and your Father who sees what is done in secret will reward you." (Matt. 6:5–6)

Don't misunderstand; Jesus wasn't denigrating public prayer. He simply wanted to warn us away from hypocrisy. The word *hypocrite*

6. William Barclay, *The Gospel of Matthew*, pp. 196–97.

comes from an ancient Greek term meaning "one behind a mask." In Greek theater, actors changed roles by changing masks—each one representing a different character. Likewise, many public prayers resembled the masks of actors in a show. "They pray for approval," Jesus said, "and in the applause of the audience, they have their reward in full" (see v. 1). But a far greater reward awaits those whose prayers are motivated by relationship with God instead of recognition from men.

Avoid Meaningless Repetition

Jesus gave a second warning about prayer: Avoid meaningless repetition.

> "And when you are praying, do not use meaningless repetition as the Gentiles do, for they suppose that they will be heard for their many words." (v. 7)

Do you remember the Baal worshipers Elijah confronted on Mount Carmel? From morning until noon they droned on, "O Baal, answer us. O Baal, answer us" (see 1 Kings 18:26). And over in Acts 19:34, the Ephesians opposed the gospel by shouting, "Great is Artemis of the Ephesians!" for two hours straight. The Gentiles commonly rattled off chant-like praises to false gods for hours on end.

But before we get too smug, we should consider what Jesus would tell evangelical Christians today. He would probably put His warning like this: "Ditch the clichés." What do we mean when we say, "Lord, thank You for Your many blessings"? What are we asking for when we say, "Be with brother Ed"? Are we merely repeating what we hear others say? What, specifically, are we thankful for? How exactly could God's presence encourage Ed? We shouldn't stop thanking God for our blessings or praying for brother Ed, but when we pray, we need to think about what we're saying instead of just regurgitating a string of meaningless jargon. God isn't impressed with words; He wants to hear what's on our hearts.

Avoid Grudges

Finally, Jesus warns us to forgive others:

> "For if you forgive others for their transgressions, your heavenly Father will also forgive you. But if you do not forgive others, then your Father will not forgive your transgressions." (Matt. 6:14–15)

Did you know your prayer life can be affected by how you relate to others? Withholding forgiveness, harboring grudges, letting relational wounds fester—all these can get in the way of a healthy prayer life, and even hinder our walks with God (see also 5:23–24; 1 John 4:20–21).

Pray to be heard by God, not applauded by people. Pray from the heart, not with meaningless repetition. And forgive others before approaching God. Pretty simple instructions, but what a difference they can make!

How Then Shall We Pray?

In addition to giving us these general principles about prayer, Jesus provided a sample, widely known as the Lord's Prayer. In addition to being an invocation we can—and should—repeat often, it also teaches us a great deal about the nature of prayer itself. Each phrase reveals an important characteristic of an effective petition that, if incorporated into church prayer, can greatly improve our corporate communication with God. "Pray, then, in this way," Jesus said:

> 'Our Father who is in heaven,
> Hallowed be Your name.
> Your kingdom come.
> Your will be done,
> On earth as it is in heaven.
> Give us this day our daily bread.
> And forgive us our debts, as we also have
>   forgiven our debtors.
> And do not lead us into temptation, but deliver us
>   from evil. For Yours is the kingdom and the
>   power and the glory forever. Amen.'
> (Matt. 6:9–13)

Let's examine each part individually.

Acknowledge Who God Is

Jesus first acknowledged God for Who He is. First, God is *our Father*. We have a close, loving, familial relationship with Him. We can even call Him "Abba," or "Daddy" (Gal. 4:6). The Lord wants to do for us what any loving father would do for his beloved children. And we should not tremble as we approach Him.

But this Father is no mere mortal—He's *in heaven.* He's the Creator and Ruler of the entire universe. He sits on the throne, knowing all things and controlling the cosmos. He's everywhere all the time. His knowledge and power are without end. While we should not tremble as we approach Him, neither should we converse with Him flippantly or without honor. A healthy dose of biblical fear, or reverence, will keep us balanced in how we view and approach Him.

In light of God's character, we should not wonder at Christ's instruction for us to call His name *hallowed,* which means "holy."

Focus on God's Plan and Purpose

Jesus next focused on God's plan and purpose. He indicated that we should ask for God's kingdom to come. This request refers to God's plan to establish a future, literal kingdom when Christ returns. When we pray for this, we acknowledge that God has a plan for humanity, that our church participates in it, and that we trust in His ability to bring it to fruition.

What are we to do in the meantime? We're to ask for God's will to be done—on earth as it is in heaven. In heaven, God's desires are carried out without question, hesitation, or confusion. Wouldn't it be great if they were carried out the same way on earth? Jesus instructs us to pray for just that.

Ask God for What You Need

Once we're sufficiently focused on God and His plan, we're then ready to present our petitions to Him. We ask Him to provide us with our "daily bread." The term for "daily," *epiousion,* means "sufficient for today."[7] So we're not asking God to give us every little whim that tickles our fancy. If we did, we'd be focused on ourselves and our own plans. Rather, we want to trust God for providing what we need to serve Him.

Confess Your Sins

Because sin hinders prayer, we ought to make confession a common feature in our communications with God. But before we lay

---

7. Louis A. Barbieri Jr., "Matthew" in *The Bible Knowledge Commentary,* New Testament edition, ed. John F. Walvoord and Roy B. Zuck (Colorado Springs, Colo.: Victor Books, Chariot Victor Publishing, 1983), p. 32.

our iniquities before Him, expecting Him to wipe them clean, we need to make sure that we've forgiven others.

The words "as we also have forgiven our debtors" are explained in verses 14 and 15, which state that God will forgive us if we forgive others but will not forgive us if we refuse to forgive others. This doesn't mean that our forgiveness earns us the right to be forgiven by God. It *does* mean that God forgives only the penitent and that evidence of true penitence is a forgiving spirit.[8]

Only by forgiving others can we kneel before God with the confidence that He'll forgive us. And only with God's forgiveness can our petitions rise unhindered to His ears. If we want Him to listen to us, we must show grace to others.

Request Deliverance from Evil

Finally, Jesus instructed us to ask God to "lead us not into temptation, but deliver us from evil" (v. 13). This seems like an odd request, doesn't it? After all, shouldn't we be able to take this one for granted? Of all the people in the universe, the three Persons of the godhead would be the last to tempt us into sin.

To pray this request properly, we need to understand it for what it is—it's a figure of speech that implies its opposite. When we ask the Lord to lead us *not* into temptation, we're asking Him to lead us *away from it*, into righteousness. We're requesting that He guide us into situations where, far from temptation, we can protect ourselves and preserve our good standing.[9] D. A. Carson reveals the special attitude behind such a request:

> This petition is a hefty reminder that, just as we ought consciously to depend on God for physical sustenance, so also ought we to sense our dependence on him for moral triumph and spiritual victory. Indeed, to fail in this regard is already to have fallen, for it is part of that ugly effort at independence which refuses to recognize our position as creatures before God. As Christians grow in holy living, they sense their own inherent moral weakness and rejoice

8. John R. W. Stott, *The Message of the Sermon on the Mount (Matthew 5–7): Christian Counter-Culture*, The Bible Speaks Today Series (Downers Grove, Ill.: InterVarsity Press, 1978), p. 149.

9. D. A. Carson, *The Sermon on the Mount* (Grand Rapids, Mich.: Baker Book House, 1978), p. 70.

that whatever virtue they possess flourishes as the fruit of the Spirit. More and more they recognize the deceptive subtleties of their own hearts, and the malicious cunning of the evil one, and fervently request of their heavenly Father, "Lead us not into temptation, but deliver us from evil."[10]

This is prayer as God intended it—simple, to the point, and honest. No formulas or schedules. No postures. Just conversation with God. But, as we've seen, there's more to it than just opening our mouths and letting it rip. Jesus has given us some helpful instructions on how to make the most of our conversations with God. All for the church. All for our benefit. All to help us make the most of our time here on earth.

 Living Insights

The church is the bride of Christ, but the Lord's Prayer reveals many other facets of our relationship with God. Go through the prayer and list the various ways in which we are related to Him.

Prayer	Relationship Revealed
"Our Father who is in heaven,	*child to father*
Hallowed be Your name.	*worshiper to God*
Your kingdom come.	
Your will be done,	
On earth as it is in heaven.	
Give us this day our daily bread.	
And forgive us our debts,	
as we also have forgiven our debtors.	
And do not lead us into temptation,	
but deliver us from evil."	

10. D. A. Carson, *The Sermon on the Mount*, p. 71.

This Living Insights section is adapted from "Prayer and Fasting Minus All the Pizzazz" in the Bible study guide *Simple Faith*, written by Ken Gire, from the Bible-teaching ministry of Charles R. Swindoll (Anaheim, Calif.: Insight for Living, 1991).

Now that you've discovered some different dimensions of your relationship with God, spend some time in prayer alone, praying through the Lord's Prayer with a new freshness. Get away to a quiet place where you can say the prayer out loud, pausing over each line and thanking Him for specific things—as a child would thank a father, as a worshiper would thank God, and so on. You might even share what you've learned with your pastor or worship leader. Your church may want to work it into its worship services.

Chapter 8

A Fresh Glimpse of Glory

Selected Scriptures

Why does the church exist? The answer may seem obvious, like the answers to "Why do we brush our teeth?" or "Why do we put gas in our cars?" No doubt you can think of several reasons off the top of your head. But have you ever really probed the Scriptures to see what they say about the purpose of the Church? You may be surprised at what you find.

Asking *why*, even about routine parts of our lives, often invigorates us. It helps us remember why we do things in the first place. It causes us to realign our focus with the desired outcome. It helps us get to the heart of an issue, compelling us to articulate our values and purpose; and it prods us to map out a course of action rather than idle along the path of least resistance.

So today, we're looking into why the church exists. What is its primary purpose? Is it

- to present the gospel to the lost?

- to bring hope to the hurting?

- to provide a place for worship and instruction?

- to equip the saints for the work of the ministry?

- to support family values?

- to prepare children for life?

- to provide for the needy?

- to stimulate action on important issues?

- to give people an opportunity to serve?

- to teach the Scriptures?

- to be a model of righteousness?

This chapter is adapted from "Our Purpose" in the Bible study guide *The Bride*, written by Gary Matlack, from the Bible-teaching ministry of Charles R. Swindoll (Anaheim, Calif.: Insight for Living, 1994).

Churches do all of these. Each of the above is valuable and necessary . . . but would you believe that not one of them captures the central reason for the church's existence?

The Purpose of the Church

In 1 Corinthians 10:31, the apostle Paul let us in on the answer.

> Whether, then, you eat or drink or whatever you do, do all to the glory of God.

That's it! The purpose of every Christian, both individually and collectively as the church, is to glorify the Lord. Whether we're eating at potlucks or bringing food to the needy, sending out missionaries or taking in teaching, the ultimate goal is God's glory. (See also 1 Cor. 6:19–20; Col. 3:17.)

This mission statement was originally written for the Corinthian church, but if you keep wandering through the pages of Scripture, you'll find similar instructions more generally directed toward God's people as a whole.

> Now may the God who gives perseverance and encouragement grant you to be of the same mind with one another according to Christ Jesus, *so that with one accord you may with one voice glorify the God and Father of our Lord Jesus Christ.* (Rom. 15:5–6, emphasis added)

And,

> Now to Him who is able to do far more abundantly beyond all that we ask or think, according to the power that works within us, to Him be the glory in the church and in Christ Jesus to all generations forever and ever. Amen. (Eph. 3:20–21)

"Church," God says, "glorify Me!" We can't miss it. It rings like wedding bells throughout the Bible. But in this day of inflated egos and Madison Avenue religion, we're tempted to drown out God's glory in the fanfare of our own pursuits. "Let's get bigger," some say. "Let's make a huge impression. How about a television ministry? We need dynamic preaching and excellent music." Such things can be part of a wonderful church ministry. But if God's glory is not the primary focus, they ring hollow.

Let's get very practical about the glory of God: it must be the underlying motive in all we do. That brings us back to those *why* questions. "Why are we building a new sanctuary? Why do I teach or sing? Why do I help in the nursery? Why have I budgeted my finances this way?" The answer should be driven by a passion for His glory.

Can you imagine fueling every action, every word, every church program with the glory of God? What would happen? Second Thessalonians reveals an interesting effect.

> To this end also we pray for you always, that our God will count you worthy of your calling, and fulfill every desire for goodness and the work of faith with power, so that the name of our Lord Jesus will be glorified in you, and you in Him, according to the grace of our God and the Lord Jesus Christ. (1:11–12)

Amazing, isn't it? As we glorify God, we are glorified in Him. Glory leads to more glory. That's what Jesus meant when He said,

> Let your light shine before men in such a way that they may see your good works, and glorify your Father who is in heaven. (Matt. 5:16; see also 1 Pet. 2:11–12)

All it takes is one person with a burning desire to glorify God. Then that flame touches off brushfires of glory that blaze across the spiritual landscape.

Do you feel as though you've unearthed this gem of insight for the first time? It may seem like a newfangled formula for successful ministry, but it's as ancient as the Scriptures. You'll even find it in the annals of church history. The *Westminster Shorter Catechism*, devised in 1647, was recited by young Scottish students who were asked by their teachers, "What is the chief end of man?" The memorized response: "Man's chief end is to glorify God, and to enjoy him forever."[1]

Three Glimpses of Glory

What exactly does it mean to glorify God, and how do we do it? Perhaps the best place to start is with the root of the word itself. The term *glory* rises from our religious vocabulary like a stray balloon.

---

1. Philip Schaff, *The Creeds of Christendom*, 4th ed., rev. and enl. (New York, N.Y.: Harper and Brothers, 1919), vol. 3, p. 676.

We sometimes let it go without thinking, without appreciating all that it means. Let's get a firm grasp on glory by examining its usage in Scripture, which reveals three different meanings.

The Presence of God

The first meaning focuses on the holy light that emanates from God.

> Then the cloud covered the tent of meeting, and the glory of the Lord filled the tabernacle. (Exod. 40:34)

When God made an appearance, the Israelites knew it. His searing light flooded the tabernacle like an exploding nova. So magnificent was His presence that to enter it inappropriately meant sudden death. Why? Because sinful, fallen people cannot stand in the physical presence of the Holy God of Israel. The light signified His literal *presence.*

The Power of God

A second and equally significant usage of glory appears in Psalm 19, where David portrayed it as a unique representation of God's *power.*

> The heavens are telling of the glory of God;
> And their expanse is declaring the work of His hand.
> (v. 1)

The glory of which the heavens speak is the glory of God's power, which He has revealed by creating and ruling over this universe in which we live. And this cosmic aspect of His glory actually reflects itself in the things He has made.

> All flesh is not the same flesh, but there is one flesh of men, and another flesh of beasts, and another flesh of birds, and another of fish. There are also heavenly bodies and earthly bodies, but the glory of the heavenly is one, and the glory of the earthly is another. There is one glory of the sun, and another glory of the moon, and another glory of the stars; for star differs from star in glory. (1 Cor. 15:39–41)

How intriguing. Glory pulses from the planets just as it flows from earthbound creatures. All of it, though, is merely a reflection. The source of the glory is God Himself, the glory of His power.

When pondering the purpose of the church, however, neither the power He displayed in creation nor the brilliance of His holy light best describes His glory.

The Preeminence of God

John the Baptizer embodied a third kind of glory—the kind the church should demonstrate. Listen to the fiery preacher's response to the self-righteous Pharisees when they questioned his motives:

> He said, "I am a voice of one crying in the wilderness, 'Make straight the way of the Lord,' as Isaiah the prophet said." Now they had been sent from the Pharisees. They asked him, and said to him, "Why then are you baptizing, if you are not the Christ, nor Elijah, nor the Prophet?" John answered them saying, "I baptize in water, but among you stands One whom you do not know. It is He who comes after me, the thongs of whose sandal I am not worthy to untie." (John 1:23–27)

John never sought the glory that belonged to the Lord Jesus Christ. In fact, when his disciples came to him later, inquiring why Jesus' ministry was flourishing, John replied, "He must increase, but I must decrease" (John 3:30).

Glory, then, as it relates to the church, means to acknowledge God's *preeminence*, to magnify and elevate the Lord as we diminish and deny ourselves. It means to occupy ourselves with and commit ourselves to His ways rather than going our own ways. As Isaiah recorded,

> "My thoughts are not your thoughts,
> Nor are your ways My ways," declares the Lord.
> "For as the heavens are higher than the earth,
> So are My ways higher than your ways
> And My thoughts than your thoughts."
> (Isa. 55:8–9)

We cannot acknowledge God's preeminence while seeking our own personal glory. That applies to all—John the Baptizer, the church, and individuals (see also Rev. 4:11).

Three Applications of Glory

"How does God's glory affect *me?*" you might ask. When it trickles down from heaven and seeps into the soil of daily living, what difference does it make? Among other things, it will change how we approach the *whens, ins* and *ifs* of life.

When I'm unsure, I glorify Him by seeking His will and waiting for His guidance—when I change careers, choose a spouse, grapple with unexpected illness, or sweep up broken dreams. God's glory ferments in the cask of seeking and waiting.

In my public and private life, God's glory reigns. In every relationship, whether pleasant or repulsive. In all my work, whether rewarded or overlooked. In secret preparation and public presentation. Whether my position is prominent or obscure, His glory reigns.

If I succeed or if I fail, God is glorified. If my spouse stays or walks away. If the cause for which I diligently campaigned fails. If my church grows or shrinks. Whether people understand or not. If I leave the ministry or stay in it, I let His glory shine.

Thoughts to Keep in Mind

Convinced of our need to glorify God yet? We've looked at *what* His glory is and *how* to achieve it. We've even addressed the question, "*Why* does the church exist?," but there is another *why* question that remains unanswered: "Why is it so important for us to glorify God?" The following thoughts ought to provide us with ample reasons:

- *The light of God's presence must illuminate our endeavors, or they're done in vain.*

- *The authority of God's power must energize our efforts, or they're doomed to fail.*

- *The significance of God's preeminence must remain paramount in our thoughts, or everything we do becomes a monument to man.*

 Living Insights

Have you ever seen a lunar eclipse? The moon passes behind the earth, directly away from the sun, and eases into the earth's shadow. For about two hours, the moon fades from view, cloaked in the earth's darkness, deprived of the sun's light.[2]

---

2. *Encyclopædia Britannica*, 15th ed., see "Eclipse, Occultation, and Transit."

Simply put, the earth gets in the way. You see, the moon generates no light of its own; it depends on the sun for illumination. When the earth blocks the sun's rays, the moon darkens and its surface cools until it emerges once again to bask in the light.

Spiritually speaking, Christians are like the moon. We bask in the Son's light, reflecting His glory. But sometimes the earth gets in the way. We start living by the world's standards—seeking glory for ourselves, leaving God out of our decisions, craving pleasure instead of piety. Then we slip into the world's shadow, hiding God's glory from others.

Have you ever been through a spiritual eclipse? Do you see one coming? Are you letting the world keep you from reflecting God's glory? Take a few minutes to think about the activities that make up a typical day in your life. Your job. Your church. The causes you support. The decisions you make. The time you spend. The people you influence. The decisions you make. The passions you pursue. What do you see?

_____

_____

_____

Who's getting the glory? You or God?

_____

_____

If you have allowed anything to come between you and the Son, make that activity a matter of prayer. Confess your preoccupation with it to God, and commit it to His glory. Let Him guide you out of the shadows and into the glorious light of His Son.

My prayer for God's glory to shine through me:

_____

_____

_____

_____

Chapter 9

THE VALUE OF VISION

Proverbs 29:18; Habakkuk 2:1–3; 2 Kings 6:8–23

In his book *Making It Happen*, Charles Paul Conn asks a searching question:

> In your own private moments of dreaming and wishing, what can you see yourself achieving?[1]

It's a good question, isn't it? So often we get wrapped up in the details of everyday life that we forget about our dreams. We let the flame of the passions God has placed in our hearts flicker and dim. But God has put those passions there for a reason—they serve the goals of His kingdom. That's why we need to step back from our busy routines, refocus our priorities, and redirect our energies. Our God-given dreams are too important to let slip away. As Conn challenges us,

> Whatever it is
> however impossible it seems
> whatever the obstacle that lies between you and it
> if it is noble
> if it is consistent with God's Kingdom, you must
> hunger after it, and stretch yourself to
> reach it.[2]

Keeping the fire stoked, though, is not easy, especially when the world around us constantly tries to smother it with wet blankets of incessant deadlines, relentless responsibilities, and mind-numbing routines. How can we keep our hearts blazing for the long run? What will fuel our spirits to achieve God's purposes?

In a word, *vision*. Vision gives us long-range perspective in the midst of short-term obstacles. It keeps us on track with God when circumstances would drive us to distraction. Where do we get our vision? In what ways can vision benefit our lives? And what happens if we try to live without it? Let's take some time to find the answers to these questions.

1. Charles Paul Conn, *Making It Happen: A Christian Looks at Money, Competition, and Success* (Old Tappan, N.J.: Fleming H. Revell Co., 1981), p. 32.

2. Conn, *Making It Happen*, p. 32.

Without Vision, We Are Lost

People who long to accomplish what God wants them to do cannot stay at the task for long without vision—clearly-defined, carefully-stated, God-given directions. In fact, we could describe vision as *a well thought-through, clearly-stated objective, given by God to His people so that they understand it and hopefully believe it and act upon it.* Yes, you read right—"hopefully." History is strewn with the wreckage of those who either weren't given the clear truth of God's Word or simply wouldn't believe and act on what they did understand.

As Proverbs 29:18 tells us,

> Where there is no vision, the people are
> unrestrained,
> But happy is he who keeps the law.

Now, the "vision" Solomon spoke of here is a revelation "granted by God to chosen messengers, i.e. prophets."[3] Basically, this verse means "that without God's Word people abandon themselves to their own sinful ways. On the other hand keeping (obeying) God's Law (cf. 28:4, 7) brings happiness."[4] Eugene Peterson gives us a helpful paraphrase:

> If people can't see what God is doing,
> they stumble all over themselves;
> But when they attend to what he reveals,
> they are most blessed.[5]

A parallel passage to Proverbs 29:18 can be found in Hosea's prophecy. In Hosea's time, the priests were failing to communicate God's ways and lead the people in the path of life. So the Lord told Hosea,

> "My people are destroyed for lack of knowledge."
> (Hos. 4:6a)

---

3. R. Laird Harris, Gleason L. Archer Jr., Bruce K. Waltke, eds., *Theological Wordbook of the Old Testament* (Chicago, Ill.: Moody Press, 1980), vol. 1, p. 275.

4. Sid S. Buzzell, "Proverbs," in *The Bible Knowledge Commentary*, Old Testament edition, ed. John F. Walvoord and Roy B. Zuck (Colorado Springs, Colo.: Chariot Victor Publishing, 1985), p. 968. Several times in the book of Judges we read that "in those days there was no king in Israel"—no divinely guided ruler—so everyone did what was right in their own eyes (17:6; 21:25; see also 18:1; 19:1). This included some of the vilest sins recorded in the Bible.

5. Eugene H. Peterson, *The Message: The Old Testament Wisdom Books in Contemporary English* (Colorado Springs, Colo.: NavPress, 1996), p. 346.

Hosea's contemporary, Micah, gave an even more graphic picture of what happens when God's messengers are not faithful in communicating God's vision:

> Now hear this, heads of the house of Jacob
> And rulers of the house of Israel,
> Who abhor justice
> And twist everything that is straight,
> Who build Zion with bloodshed
> And Jerusalem with violent injustice.
> Her leaders pronounce judgment for a bribe,
> Her priests instruct for a price
> And her prophets divine for money.
> Yet they lean on the Lord saying,
> "Is not the Lord in our midst?
> Calamity will not come upon us."
> Therefore, on account of you
> Zion will be plowed as a field,
> Jerusalem will become a heap of ruins,
> And the mountain of the temple will become
>   high places of a forest. (Mic. 3:9–12)

What we need, then, is to keep God's revealed will always in our sight, always in our mind, always in our heart. When His vision becomes our vision, we leave the path of destruction and walk in the way of blessing.

With Vision, We Gain New Strength

Two Old Testament prophets, Habakkuk and Elisha, show us that when the eyes of our faith are focused on the reliability of God's awesome character and power, we will gain new strength to persevere in what He has called us to do—no matter what our surrounding circumstances look like.

Habakkuk

Habakkuk was called to be God's prophet during the last, dark days of Judah. His fellow messenger during that era was Jeremiah, known as the Weeping Prophet, which gives us some idea of how bad the times were. The young, godly King Josiah had died in battle, and his son, Jehoahaz, began a three-month reign of evil. Pharaoh Neco put an end to his kingship, imprisoning him in Egypt, where he died. Another of Josiah's sons, Jehoiakim, then ascended the throne at the pharaoh's direction and plunged the little remnant kingdom into a head-spinning moral descent (see 2 Kings 23:29–24:4).

Dismayed by the unfaithfulness, wickedness, and injustice that seemed to go unchecked, Habakkuk cried out to God:

> How long, O Lord, will I call for help,
> And You will not hear?
> I cry out to You, "Violence!"
> Yet You do not save.
> Why do You make me see iniquity,
> And cause me to look on wickedness?
> Yes, destruction and violence are before me;
> Strife exists and contention arises.
> Therefore the law is ignored
> And justice is never upheld.
> For the wicked surround the righteous;
> Therefore justice comes out perverted.
> (Hab. 1:2–4)

At the heart of his complaint, Habakkuk was asking, *Are you really in control, Lord? Will You ever put things right?* To these poignant questions, God gave a disturbing answer: Yes, He would judge Judah for her sins—but He would use the cruel, pagan Babylonians to do it (vv. 5–11). Habakkuk was stunned:

> Why are You silent when the wicked swallow up
> Those more righteous than they? . . .
> [Will they] continually slay nations without
>   sparing? (vv. 13b, 17b)

Unable to fathom God's ways, Habakkuk decided to wait silently and attentively to see what God would do next:

> I will stand on my guard post
> And station myself on the rampart;
> And I will keep watch to see what
> He will speak to me. (2:1a)

God then answered him with another revelation: merciless Babylon herself would be judged without mercy (vv. 4–19). "Record the vision," the Lord told His prophet,

> "And inscribe it on tablets,

That the one who reads it may run.
For the vision is yet for the appointed time;
It hastens toward the goal and it will not fail.
Though it tarries, wait for it;
For it will certainly come, it will not delay."
(vv. 2b–3)

"History *is* in My hands, and My purposes *will not* be thwarted," God reassured Habakkuk—and reassures us. The world may not look like it's ruled by God and that He will win the final victory, but that tells more about the limitations of our human eyesight than it does about God's sovereignty. God would have us sharpen our spiritual sight, trust in what He has revealed to us in His Word, and persevere in what He has called us to be and to do. He sums this up to Habakkuk in the pivotal verse of the book:

"The righteous will live by his faith." (v. 4b)

Centuries later, the apostle Paul reminded us of this same truth: "For we walk by faith, not by sight" (2 Cor. 5:7; see also 4:17–18). Because God revealed His long-range plan to Habakkuk, the prophet's faith was stabilized and he could hold on to hope in a world gone awry. Aren't we glad Habakkuk took the message not only to his people, but also to everyone who has read his words throughout time? This vision of the certainty of God's justice and righteousness can keep us going too, so we can say along with Habakkuk,

Though the fig tree should not blossom
And there be no fruit on the vines,
Though the yield of the olive should fail
And the fields produce no food,
Though the flock should be cut off from the fold
And there be no cattle in the stalls,
Yet I will exult in the Lord,
I will rejoice in the God of my salvation.
The Lord God is my strength,
And He has made my feet like hinds' feet,
And makes me walk on my high places.
(Hab. 3:17–19)

Elisha

Like Habakkuk, Elisha was also God's ray of light to a spiritually darkened nation. Elisha ministered to the northern kingdom of

Israel more than two hundred years before Habakkuk's time. Unfortunately, where the southern kingdom of Judah knew blessed periods of revival under eight righteous kings, Israel was in chronic rebellion against God under one wicked king after another. What a testimony to God's grace, though, that He still sent prophets to call His covenanted people back to Him. Despite their waywardness, God continued to look on His people with love and compassion. Elisha's ministry provides a window into this aspect of God's heart.

In 2 Kings 6:8, we find the king of Aram making raids on Israel—or at least trying to make raids. He wasn't having much success because God kept revealing his secret plans to Elisha, who in turn warned Israel's King Joram, who wisely guarded himself against the enemy attacks (vv. 9–10). The king of Aram was understandably frustrated and wondered if he had an informant in his camp. But no mere human scheming was thwarting the king's plans. One of his servants, possibly aware of what Elisha had done for Naaman (see 5:1–14), told the king,

> "Elisha, the prophet who is in Israel, tells the king
> of Israel the words that you speak in your bedroom."
> (6:12)

Incensed, the king ordered his troops to go by night and surround the town where Elisha lived and get that prophet (vv. 13–14)! The next morning, Elisha's servant received a jarring wake-up call.

> Now when the attendant of the man of God had
> risen early and gone out, behold, an army with
> horses and chariots was circling the city. And his
> servant said to him, "Alas, my master! What shall
> we do?" (v. 15)

Calming his terrified servant, Elisha replied,

> "Do not fear, for those who are with us are more than
> those who are with them." (v. 16; compare Ps. 27;
> 1 John 4:4)

The servant must have wondered if Elisha had had one too many visions—*Who is with us? I don't see anybody but the two of us.* But Elisha wasn't hallucinating. His spiritual eyes were wide open to God's protection, and he kindly prayed that his servant would see what he saw too:

> Then Elisha prayed and said, "O Lord, I pray, open

his eyes that he may see." And the Lord opened the servant's eyes and he saw; and behold, the mountain was full of horses and chariots of fire all around Elisha. (2 Kings 6:17)

A vastly more powerful angelic army outnumbered Aram's now meager-looking forces, and the servant's fear was replaced with courage. Commentator Matthew Henry observes, "The opening of our eyes will be the silencing of our fears. In the dark we are most apt to be frightened. The clearer sight we have of the sovereignty and power of heaven the less we shall fear the calamities of this earth."[6]

The sovereignty of God, however, would initially be a little less comforting for the Aramean army. In contrast to his prayer that his servant's eyes be opened, Elisha prayed that God would blind the invading army (v. 18). The prophet then led them to Israel's capital, Samaria, where the surrounders' eyes were opened and they saw that they had become the surrounded (vv. 19–20). Reflecting the Lord's merciful kindness, Elisha told King Joram to spare his enemies' lives and instead give them a feast and send them home in peace (vv. 21–23a). What was the divinely arranged outcome?

The marauding bands of Arameans did not come again into the land of Israel. (v. 23b)

With his eyes firmly fixed on God's power and protection, Elisha was able to be God's agent of peace and spare many lives from the ravages of war.

Vision's Ultimate Value: We Have Hope

Why should we study the stories of these prophets? What does ancient history have to do with our lives today? Listen to what the Holy Spirit told Paul:

Whatever was written in earlier times was written for our instruction, so that through perseverance and the encouragement of the Scriptures we might have hope. (Rom. 15:4)

These Old Testament stories are about today's hope—yesterday's

6. Matthew Henry, *Commentary on the Whole Bible*, one-volume edition, ed. Leslie F. Church (Grand Rapids, Mich.: Zondervan Publishing House, Regency Reference Library, 1961), p. 408.

victories are about tomorrow's dreams! God has given us these stories to instruct us, to help us persevere, to encourage us, and to fuel us with hope.

Habakkuk's book, for example, reassures us that right will triumph over wrong, and that God still watches over those who persevere for His cause. The vision God gave Habakkuk also cleared away his confusion and brought him clarity and stability—and it can do the same for us.

The episode from Elisha's life encourages us that God's power is greater than any human obstacle, and that His protection is surer than any safe route we can come up with. We can also learn from Elisha's servant that when our eyes are open to God's work, we can gain courage, just as he did.

Are you willing to persevere in the vision God has given you? Are you ready to hold fast to hope as you live for Christ in a world that is blind to Him? It won't be easy; God doesn't do all the work for us. Noah had to construct that ark; Nehemiah had to rebuild that wall. But the hope of a God-given new beginning kept them going in the face of all kinds of obstacles and opposition, until they knew the joy of accomplishing God's plans as partners with Him.

So whatever dream or vision God has given you, whatever aspect of His Word fires your passion, follow it with your whole heart. Lean into the chill winds that will inevitably come your way, and keep pressing on. And remember the great vision that God has called us all to:

> Whatever you do in word or deed, do all in the name
> of the Lord Jesus, giving thanks through Him to God
> the Father. (Col. 3:17)

 Living Insights

What vision has God given you? It may or may not be scaling Mount Everest, kayaking around the world, or orbiting Mars. It may or may not be winning the war on drugs, banning nuclear weapons, or banishing poverty and hunger from the earth. Your dream may be as grand as these, or it may be simpler—though not always easier—such as running a successful business with honesty and integrity, building a home with love and faithfulness, or raising children with compassion and joy.

What dream has God put on your heart?

_____

_____

_____

_____

How are you doing in the pursuit of this dream? Are energy and excitement still filling your sails, or have obstacles, setbacks, and distractions edged you into the doldrums? Or have pressing concerns eclipsed your vision entirely, dragging you off-course? Write down your progress in pursuing this dream, and be as specific as possible about what has brought you to this place.

_____

_____

_____

_____

If your energy is unflagging, that's great! You probably have a very clear, long-range view. To help you keep that in focus, write down what it is that keeps you going. Try to identify that star by which you steer your ship.

_____

_____

_____

_____

If your sails have drooped and discouragement has set in, take some time now to recall your original goals and purposes. What do you think God was calling you to accomplish?

_____

_____

_____

_____

What needs to change to get you back on track? Do you need to shift some of your priorities? Do you need to spend more time in God's Word to remember what He has called you to, first and foremost, as a Christian? Do you need to spend more time resting in prayer and less time in a do-it-yourself mode? Take some time to sit down with the Lord and strategize what you need to do.

Paul gave us a good word to live by when he told us to do all that we do in the name of the Lord Jesus (Col. 3:17). As you refocus on the vision God has set before you and gather new energy to pursue it, take along another good word from Paul:

> Walk in a manner worthy of the Lord, to please Him in all respects, bearing fruit in every good work and increasing in the knowledge of God. (Col. 1:10)

Chapter 10

THE ONE
IRRESISTIBLE APPEAL

John 13:34–35; 1 Corinthians 13:1–3

How are we recognized as true followers of Christ? By the crosses we wear around our necks? By the little fish, the *ichthus*, affixed to our bumpers? By the version of the Bible we read, or the type of clothing we wear—or don't wear? In John 13:34–35, Jesus told us the one distinguishing characteristic of true followers:

> "A new commandment I give to you, that you love one another, even as I have loved you, that you also love one another. *By this all men will know that you are My disciples*, if you have love for one another." (John 13:34–35, emphasis added)

No matter what denomination we belong to, no matter what kind of icons we attach to ourselves or our possessions, no matter what we look like, there exists only one defining attribute of a true disciple of Christ: love.

But God intended His love to be poured out not only through our personal lives, but also through our churches. In his touching book entitled *Afterglow*, Sherwood Wirt writes,

> I have learned there is no point in talking about strong churches and weak churches. Such categories are unrealistic and beside the point. There are only loving churches and unloving churches.[1]

We so often get distracted with the latest growth strategies and programs that we forget the one thing that can make us irresistible to the world—our love. With this thought in mind, let's examine the kind of love God wants us to exhibit, and begin by looking at the One who was our perfect model of love: Jesus Christ.

---

1. Attributed to Sherwood Wirt by Charles R. Swindoll in the sermon "The One Irresistible Appeal" at Stonebriar Community Church, October 17, 1999.

Jesus: Our Model of Love

Have you ever noticed that we tend to go easier on the shortcomings of our friends than on those of strangers? Think about it. A rude comment or a bad attitude from a stranger makes our tempers flare. The same comment from someone we love, however, is much more tolerable. Why? Because it's balanced by all the good qualities we've experienced in that person. In other words, we take their shortcomings in context.

Jesus, however, treated strangers with just as much understanding as He did His closest friends. Look at how He responded to one especially offensive young stranger:

> As He was setting out on a journey, a man ran up to Him and knelt before Him, and asked Him, "Good Teacher, what shall I do to inherit eternal life?" And Jesus said to him, "Why do you call Me good? No one is good except God alone. You know the commandments, 'Do not murder, Do not commit adultery, Do not steal, Do not bear false witness, Do not defraud, Honor your father and mother.'" And he said to Him, "Teacher, I have kept all these things from my youth up." Looking at him, Jesus felt a love for him and said to him, "One thing you lack: go and sell all you possess and give to the poor, and you will have treasure in heaven; and come, follow Me." But at these words he was saddened, and he went away grieving, for he was one who owned much property. (Mark 10:17–22)

Did you detect the hint of arrogance in the young man's words? He couldn't possibly have kept all the commandments all his life. He possessed everything the world had to offer: wealth, prestige, power. Now he wanted to acquire the one thing he was lacking—eternal life—and for this he sought the advice of Jesus, Whom he regarded not as the Savior, but as a mere teacher. It had to be insulting. This rich young ruler not only neglected to acknowledge Jesus' position, but he cheapened His most priceless commodity by reducing it to something that could be purchased without sacrifice. But Jesus still "felt a love for him."

Jesus demonstrated love, going so far as to lay down His very life for the world (John 15:13), but He also talked about it:

> [A lawyer] asked Him a question, testing Him, "Teacher, which is the great commandment in the Law?" And He said to him, "'You shall love the Lord your God with all your heart, and with all your soul, and with all your mind.' This is the great and foremost commandment. The second is like it, 'You shall love your neighbor as yourself.' On these two commandments depend the whole Law and the Prophets." (Matt. 22:35–40)[2]

Jesus taught that true, godly love shows itself both vertically and horizontally. And He never omitted the horizontal aspect— not even when the people around Him were betraying and crucifying Him. But how does Jesus expect His love to manifest itself through us? He gave the disciples a practical example: He became their servant. At the Last Supper, He

> got up from supper, and laid aside His garments; and taking a towel, He girded Himself. Then He poured water into the basin, and began to wash the disciples' feet and to wipe them with the towel with which He was girded. So He came to Simon Peter. He said to Him, "Lord, do you wash my feet?" Jesus answered and said to him, "What I do you do not realize now, but you will understand hereafter." Peter said to Him, "Never shall You wash my feet!" Jesus answered him, "If I do not wash you, you have no part with Me." Simon Peter said to Him, "Lord, then wash not only my feet, but also my hands and my head." Jesus said to him, "He who has bathed needs only to wash his feet, but is completely clean; and you are clean . . ." (John 13:4–9)

Jesus demonstrated that loving one another means serving one another. John, who was present for this lesson, later elaborated on this theme:

> We know that we have passed out of death into life, because we love the brethren. He who does not love

2. Also recorded in Mark 12:28–31.

abides in death. . . . We know love by this, that He laid down His life for us; and we ought to lay down our lives for the brethren. But whoever has the world's goods, and sees his brother in need and closes his heart against him, how does the love of God abide in him? Little children, let us not love with word or with tongue, but in deed and truth. (1 John 3:14, 16–18)

John told us that love is not only a *noun*; it's a *verb* as well. But the grammar of love doesn't end with Christ's immediate disciples. Paul, too, taught it:

For you were called to freedom, brethren; only do not turn your freedom into an opportunity for the flesh, *but through love serve one another.* (Gal. 5:13, emphasis added)

General Observations about Love

Since action-oriented love is so important and so prominently taught by Scripture, let's look at the greatest exposition ever written on the subject, found in 1 Corinthians 13. We'll look at the specific characteristics of love in the next few chapters. For now, let's just draw some general observations from Paul's opening remarks:

If I speak with the tongues of men and of angels, but do not have love, I have become a noisy gong or a clanging cymbal. If I have the gift of prophecy, and know all mysteries and all knowledge; and if I have all faith, so as to remove mountains, but do not have love, I am nothing. And if I give all my possessions to feed the poor, and if I surrender my body to be burned, but do not have love, it profits me nothing. (vv. 1–3)

In these three verses, Paul revealed just how important love is to the church. He used five conditional statements to compare love to a list of other spiritual endeavors. Look at some of his words again, this time in list form:

- *If* I speak with the tongues of men and of angels . . .

- *If* I have the gift of prophecy, and know all mysteries and all knowledge . . .

- *If* I have all faith, so as to remove mountains . . .
- *If* I give all my possessions to feed the poor . . .
- *If* I deliver my body to be burned . . .

What a list! Were someone to accomplish just one of these feats, most of us would consider him or her worthy of induction into the Spiritual Hall of Fame! What could possibly compare with such giftedness and sacrifice?

"Not so fast," Paul said, as he tacked on the reminder that even the most impressive achievements are pointless without love. Look at the conclusion he cited three times in his list:

- If I speak with the tongues of men and of angels, but do not have love, *I have become a noisy gong or a clanging cymbal.*

- If I have the gift of prophecy, and know all mysteries and all knowledge; and if I have all faith, so as to remove mountains, but do not have love, *I am nothing.*

- And if I give all my possessions to feed the poor, and if I surrender my body to be burned, but do not have love, *it profits me nothing.*

How important is love? Without it, our words rattle and clang like noisy instruments. Our display of spiritual gifts is just a show. And personal sacrifice—even martyrdom at the stake—is worthless without love's motivation. We can reduce Paul's thoughts in these first three verses to one simple formula:

Anything - Love = Nothing

Love is the only attribute that truly distinguishes us as followers of Jesus Christ—and it's the only irresistible appeal we have to offer to the world. In the following chapters, we'll examine the specific characteristics of love. For now, however, let's just remember to keep it at the top of our priority list.

 Living Insights

What's the greatest risk you've ever taken? Starting your own business? Investing in pork futures? Skydiving? Bungee jumping? Ice climbing?

How about loving someone?

Love is risky, isn't it? It requires us to expose our hearts to others, sometimes with agonizing results. Some people would rather run into an F-5 tornado than open themselves up to that kind of danger.

But as C. S. Lewis observed, trying to protect ourselves from the risks of love means withdrawing from life:

> There is no safe investment. To love at all is to be vulnerable. Love anything, and your heart will certainly be wrung and possibly broken. If you want to make sure of keeping it intact, you must give your heart to no one, not even to an animal. Wrap it carefully round with hobbies and little luxuries; avoid all entanglements; lock it up safe in the casket or coffin of your selfishness. But in that casket—safe, dark, motionless, airless—it will change. It will not be broken; it will become unbreakable, impenetrable, irredeemable. The alternative to tragedy, or at least to the risk of tragedy, is damnation. The only place outside Heaven where you can be perfectly safe from all the dangers and perturbations of love is Hell.[3]

You see, there are worse things than the painful potential of love. C. S. Lewis would go so far as to say that if we don't love, we run the risk of spiritual death.

Are you taking risks for the sake of Christ? Be honest. When did you last leap out of your comfort zone to get closer to someone at church? Are you taking the initiative to reach out to people you know by name and face only?

Think of one person you might show more love to this week. How will you do it?

Name: _____

Plan of action: _____

_____

_____

This Living Insight is adapted from "It's Not a Meal Without Love" in the Bible study guide *Koinōnia*, written by Gary Matlack, from the Bible-teaching ministry of Charles R. Swindoll (Anaheim, Calif.: Insight for Living, 1995), pp. 13–14.

3. C. S. Lewis, *The Four Loves* (San Diego, Calif.: Harcourt Brace Jovanovich, 1960), p. 169.

_____

_____

_____

_____

_____

_____

Now untie that heart, and take it out of its box. Sure, it's scary, but Christ has called us to do nothing less. And He'll always be there to mend us if we get hurt.

Chapter 11

FINE-TUNING YOUR LOVE LIFE

Romans 12:9–13; 1 Corinthians 13:4–5a

In the last chapter, we discovered the important role love plays in the life of the Christian and in the life of the church. We realized that love is the only defining characteristic of a true follower of Christ and that it is the one irresistible appeal the church has to offer the world. We saw how Jesus modeled action-oriented love, and how His followers, particularly John and Paul, embraced the servant-like love He taught them. Ultimately, we learned that any and all good works, minus love, amount to nothing.

One thing we did *not* do, however, was try to define love—and there's a very good reason for that. Have you ever tried to define love? It can be like trying to grab a fistful of rain. We know love is real—our hearts soak it up like a cotton shirt sops up a spring shower, and its absence leaves us parched and thirsty. Yet a compact, easy-to-grasp definition eludes us. Love, it seems, is easier to detect than define.

Maybe that's why writers throughout history have chosen to describe love in terms of how it looks and feels rather than attempt to crystallize its essence. Shakespeare once described love as a capricious thing changes like the weather:

> O, how this spring of love resembleth
> The uncertain glory of an April day,
> Which now shows all the beauty of the sun,
> And by and by a cloud takes all away![1]

H. L. Mencken said, "To be in love is merely to be in a state of perpetual anaesthesis—to mistake an ordinary young man for a

---

Parts of this chapter are adapted from "It's Not a Meal Without Love" in the Bible study guide *Koinōnia: A Recipe for Authentic Fellowship*, written by Gary Matlack, from the Bible-teaching ministry of Charles R. Swindoll (Anaheim, Calif.: Insight for Living, 1995), pp. 8–13.

1. William Shakespeare, *The Two Gentlemen of Verona*, in *William Shakespeare: The Complete Works* (London, England: Michael O'Mara Books, 1988), p. 25.

Greek god or an ordinary young woman for a goddess."[2] Montaigne regarded love as "nothing save an insatiate thirst to enjoy a greedily desired object."[3]

Do these descriptions, though, sound like the kind of love Jesus had for His disciples and us? No. Jesus' love was an others-centered activity, not a self-satisfying emotion. Augustine, who knew God and His Word, provided us with a more accurate depiction of Christian love.

> What does love look like? It has the hands to help others. It has the feet to hasten to the poor and needy. It has eyes to see misery and want. It has the ears to hear the sighs and sorrows of men. That is what love looks like.[4]

Now that sounds more like it! But let's not stop with Augustine. His description of love is good and helpful, but it's not inspired. Let's go to the Bible to see how the Holy Spirit, through Paul, describes this all-important part of Christian and church life.

The Primacy of Love

What better place to start looking at Paul's definition of love than in his *magnum opus*—the epistle to the Romans. Paul began the twelfth chapter with the word "therefore." This term, however, is no ordinary "therefore." Robert Mounce explains:

> The "therefore" in v. 1 refers back not simply to the previous argument about God's mercy in bringing salvation to Jew and Gentile *but to everything that Paul had been teaching from the beginning of the epistle.* It marks the transition from the theology of God's redemptive act in Christ Jesus to the ethical expectations that flow logically from that theological base. We come now to what is usually called the "practical" section of Romans. (emphasis added)[5]

2. H. L. Mencken, as quoted in *Dictionary of Quotations*, Bergen Evans (New York, N.Y.: Avenel Books, 1968), p. 404.

3. Montaigne, as quoted in *Dictionary of Quotations*, p. 405.

4. Augustine, as quoted in *Quote Unquote*, comp. Lloyd Cory (Wheaton, Ill.: Scripture Press Publications, Victor Books, 1977), p. 187.

5. Robert H. Mounce, *Romans*, The New American Commentary Series, vol. 27 (Nashville, Tenn.: Broadman and Holman Publishers, 1995), p. 230.

Paul spent the first eleven chapters of Romans laying a strong theological foundation, upon which he then built a structure of the Christian life in the last five chapters. How long did it take Paul to get to love once he started building this structure in chapter 12? Not long at all:

> Let love be without hypocrisy. Abhor what is evil; cling to what is good. Be devoted to one another in brotherly love; give preference to one another in honor; not lagging behind in diligence, fervent in spirit, serving the Lord; rejoicing in hope, persevering in tribulation, devoted to prayer, contributing to the needs of the saints, practicing hospitality. (vv. 9–13)

Authentic love, Paul said, causes us to be genuine, devoted, humble, diligent, and fervent. It compels us to serve the Lord, to contribute to the needs of others, and to be hospitable. Sounds a lot like Augustine's description, doesn't it? And the similarities don't stop at their descriptions. Both Paul and Augustine placed the highest priority on love. The fact that Paul turned so quickly to it reveals how highly he esteemed it among the Christian virtues. To him, it was primary.

Love in Action

Because love is so important, Paul took the time to describe it in great detail in his first letter to the Corinthians. Let's take a moment to pick up where we left off in the last lesson, to sit at Paul's feet again and listen to what he had to say about the fine points of Christian love in chapter 13.

> Love is patient, love is kind and is not jealous; love does not brag and is not arrogant, does not act unbecomingly. (1 Cor. 13:4–5a)

Each time Paul used the word *love* in 1 Corinthians 13, the Greek word is *agape*. The writers of the New Testament borrowed the term from Greek society and endowed it with a meaning more descriptive of Christ and His church. Commentators Curtis Vaughan and Thomas Lea explain:

> The verb form (*agapaō*) was used in secular writings, but it had a connotation that was somewhat cold and colorless. "Esteem" might best express its meaning.

The New Testament writers, however, took this word and gave it a full, rich meaning. They made it, in fact, the distinctive New Testament word for love. It has nothing to do with lust, nor is it mere affection. It is self-giving love, involving the direction of the will.[6]

Though this love comes from our emotions, it also involves our minds—which are prompted by the indwelling Holy Spirit. To help us get a handle on this godlike quality, we can say that *agape* seeks the highest good of another person; it wants that person's best and compels us to do what we can to help him or her reach it.

Want to know what this kind of love looks like, so you can recognize it more readily and give it away more freely? Look at how Paul described it.

Love Is Patient

Patient, in its Greek form, means "long-suffering or forbearing."[7] A long fuse, in other words. Love is slow to anger—able to handle interruptions, disappointments, and even mistreatment without exploding. *Agape* remains sensitive to people, even when they get between us and our goals.

Love Is Kind

The Greek root of the word *kind* means "useful, gracious"[8] and suggests gentle behavior. Jesus used a closely-related term in Matthew 11:30 when He said, "My yoke is *easy*, and My burden is light" (emphasis added). Love relieves—it never oppresses. It's caring—not condemning. It doesn't push people around like a schoolyard bully. It is tender, pleasant, gentle, eager to help.

The position of *kind* in relation to *patient* suggests an interesting relationship between the two terms. Commentator Gordon Fee explains:

> These first two clauses . . . represent respectively

6. Curtis Vaughan and Thomas D. Lea, *1 Corinthians*, Bible Study Commentary Series (Grand Rapids, Mich.: Zondervan Publishing House, Lamplighter Books, 1983), pp. 133–34.

7. Gerhard Kittel and Gerhard Friedrich, eds., *Theological Dictionary of the New Testament*, translated and abridged by Geoffrey W. Bromiley, (1985; reprint, Grand Rapids, Mich.: William B. Eerdmans Publishing Company, 1988), p. 551.

8. Archibald Thomas Robertson, *Word Pictures of the New Testament* (Grand Rapids, Mich.: Baker Book House, 1931), vol. 4, p. 177.

love's necessary passive and active responses toward others. The one pictures long forbearance toward them—indeed, it is difficult to improve on the KJV's "suffereth long"; the second pictures active goodness in their behalf. In Pauline theology they represent the two sides of the divine attitude toward mankind (cf. Rom. 2:4). On the one hand, God's loving forbearance is demonstrated by his holding back his wrath toward human rebellion; on the other hand, his kindness is found in the thousandfold expressions of his mercy. Thus Paul's description of love begins with this twofold description of God, who through Christ has shown himself forbearing and kind toward those who deserve divine judgment. The obvious implication, of course, is that this is how his people are to be toward others.[9]

Having established this divine implication, Paul pressed onward.

Love Is Not Jealous

The Greek root of the word *jealous* carries both positive and negative connotations. Paul used the term positively in 1 Corinthians 12:31, when he said, "But *earnestly* desire the greater gifts" (emphasis added). Here in 13:4, though, he used the negative sense, meaning to "be filled with jealousy, envy."[10] Paul could have been condemning the rivalry that existed between the Corinthians over their teachers. More than likely, he also directed these words toward some of the teachers who were seeking to undermine his teaching and win the affection of the community away from him (see 4:18).[11]

Jealousy and envy are similar but have subtle differences, both of which are implied in Paul's use of the phrase. Jealousy selfishly holds on to what it has, while envy lustfully longs for what it does not possess. These attitudes eat away at fellowship like acid. Can you

9. Gordon D. Fee, *The First Epistle to the Corinthians*, The New International Commentary on the New Testament Series (Grand Rapids, Mich.: William B. Eerdmans Publishing Company, 1987), pp. 636–37.

10. Walter Bauer, *A Greek-English Lexicon of the New Testament and Other Early Christian Literature*, 2d ed. Revised and augmented by F. Wilbur Gingrich and Fredrick W. Danker, from Walter Bauer's 5th ed., 1958 (Chicago, Ill.: University of Chicago Press, 1979), p. 338.

11. The "arrogant" persons referred to in 4:18–19 were teachers in the Corinthian church who were opposed to Paul.

imagine how different Acts 2:42–47 would read if those early believers had been jealous of one another? Instead of having "all things in common" (v. 44), they would have wanted all things for themselves.

Love Does Not Brag

Love "vaunteth not itself," says the old King James Version. Gordon D. Fee explains that,

> This rare word means literally to "behave as a braggart," or "be a windbag." It suggests self-centered actions in which there is an inordinate desire to call attention to oneself. Although Paul's use of the word is often viewed as his being critical of the desire on the part of some Corinthians to have the more "showy gifts," more likely it again reflects those in the community who are especially Paul's "rivals." [12]

Whatever a person's specific case may be, it is not possible to love and brag at the same time. Boasting indicates that a person wants others to think highly of him or her, whether deserving or not. Love, on the other hand, cares little for attention or affirmation, but only for the welfare of others and the community as a whole. Love avoids making a vain display of its own worth and accomplishments. It isn't motivated by recognition; rather, it thrives as well backstage as it does in the spotlight.

Love Is Not Arrogant

Picture someone puffed up like a bellows.[13] That's what the Greek word for *arrogance* suggests. Believers bloated with the wind of their own abilities, accomplishments, and possessions make poor parishioners. Pride keeps them from seeing beyond their own inflated chests, while many around them may be struggling for breath. Arrogance fosters division, not unity, as Paul pointed out to the Corinthians whose pride was unraveling the fiber of their fellowship (see 1 Cor. 4:6–7).

Love Does Not Act Unbecomingly

The Greek word for *act unbecomingly* appears only one other time in the New Testament—in this same letter (7:36). There Paul

---

12. Fee, *The First Epistle to the Corinthians*, p. 637.

13. Robertson, *Word Pictures*, p. 178.

employed the term to instruct a father to allow his daughter to marry if he feels that prohibiting her will drive her to act unbecomingly— in other words, to engage in sexual behavior that would displease God and would disrespect herself.

In short, love means we behave properly. We treat others—and ourselves—with respect. We use words infused with both truth and tact. We practice empathy when relating to others. If we must confront, we do so with sensitivity. Integrity should saturate our relationships. Love compels us to do the right thing.

Are you beginning to grasp what Christian love is all about? Don't try to define it. Attempts to reduce it to a Webster's-type description will only frustrate you. Rather, try to see it as Paul described it—as a picture with many different brushstrokes consisting of various colors and hues. Once you begin to see what love looks like, then you can begin painting your version of it upon the canvas of your own life.

 Living Insights

We've just begun to study the different aspects of godly love, but that doesn't mean it's too early to start applying what we've learned. Now is a good time to begin to build more *agape* into your life. Look over the characteristics of love covered in this chapter, and think about how you can integrate them into your relationships— the ones at church as well as those at home and work. Then jot down your ideas of how they can be applied to each person.

Spouse: _____

_____

Child: _____

_____

Parent: _____

_____

Friend: _____

_____

Coworker: _____

_____

Pastor: _____

_____

Sunday School teacher: _____

_____

Other members of your church: _____

_____

Chapter 12

LOOKING FOR LOVE?
START HERE!

1 Corinthians 13:5b

What is the opposite of love? Chances are, most people would say hate. Look at all the demonstrations of hatred in the world today: the ruthless killing in Bosnia, the deplorable treatment of women in the Middle East, the bone-chilling human rights violations in China, and the persecution and martyrdom of Christians worldwide. There certainly doesn't seem to be any love connected with these things! So we can see how hatred could be called the opposite of love.

But other people have answered the question differently. For example, the famous psychologist Rollo May once said,

> Hate is not the opposite of love. Apathy is.[1]

At first this comment seems odd because apathy and love have no connection at all. But that's the very point. What happens to people whose passionate love goes unrequited? Do they say, "Oh well, that's okay. Maybe I'll have better luck next time." Absolutely not! Even emotionally healthy people struggle against feelings of rage and revenge—not because they no longer love the person who has rejected them, but precisely because they still do. It's not until a spurned lover feels apathetic toward the other that they can say they've "gotten over it." So apathy could also be considered the opposite of love.

And May wasn't the only one who felt this way. George Bernard Shaw observed,

> The worst sin toward any fellow creature is to ignore him.[2]

Ignoring him is worse than pillaging his village? Worse than beating and killing him? According to Shaw, yes!

1. Source unknown.

2. Source unknown.

If you're starting to feel a little warm under the collar, don't get up to adjust the thermostat just yet. It could be that you, like most normal people, feel offended by this observation when faced with it for the first time. Why? Because it implies that people who don't regularly do good deeds are no better than those who do bad deeds, that the average Joe is just as bad as a murderer or tyrant. You probably haven't gone on a hacking spree in Rwanda or sat behind a sniper's rifle in Bosnia, but you probably *have* ignored the desperation of needy people around you, just as all of us have. And to equate mere negligence with the brutality of thugs and criminals seems outrageous—and enraging!

But consider this: the Bible places just as much blame on sins of omission as it does on sins of commission. Nowhere does it say that the latter is worse than the former. Although the results and consequences of the two may be different, both cause damage and are equally wrong in the eyes of God.

Faced with this fact, we can conclude one thing: negligence is just as sinful and destructive as outright brutality. Apathy is no better than hatred; searing rage is no worse than cool indifference. With this in mind, let's redouble our efforts to understand and practice the love that God has made available to us, not only to keep us from becoming brutal, but also to compel us to become more active in our love and care toward others.

Reminders of What Love Looks Like

Before we go on, let's make sure that we understand love the way Scripture presents it by revisiting the picture Paul began to paint in our last chapter.

> Love is patient—has a long fuse.
> Love is kind—gracious, tender, helpful.
> Love is not jealous—not possessive or envious.
> Love does not brag—avoids magnifying itself.
> Love is not arrogant—not puffed up with pride.
> Love does not act unbecomingly—behaves properly.

In addition to these qualities, we noted that love seeks the highest good for other people, that it wants what's best for them and does whatever it can to help them reach it. It always acts in truth and honesty, in humility and integrity.

Love in Action

With the full image of *agape* beginning to take shape in our minds, let's continue with the rest of the apostle's description.

Love Does Not Seek Its Own

Love "does not seek the things of itself," is the literal translation of this phrase. Love doesn't have to get its own way or occupy first place to be happy. Love is satisfied letting someone else have the seat with the best view. If someone else snatches the biggest piece of chicken from the bucket, love doesn't mind. Love rejoices when it hears of a friend's promotion. When others are right, love admits it—because it isn't driven by a compulsion to win every argument. In fact, love longs to see others succeed (1 Cor. 10:24, 33). This is the kind of love Paul wrote about when he penned these words:

> Do nothing from selfishness or empty conceit, but with humility of mind regard one another as more important than yourselves; do not merely look out for your own personal interests, but also for the interests of others. (Phil. 2:3–4)

Love Is Not Provoked

To be *provoked*, in the Greek, means to have a "sharpness of spirit."[3] As one interpretation suggests, love "is not irritable or touchy, is not quick to take offense."[4] Love can live with the unpleasantness of others without becoming unpleasant itself—which is essential for church life, considering that even the best churches are filled with imperfect people. Want to know the key to making this happen? Solomon provided the answer:

> He who conceals a transgression seeks love,
> But he who repeats a matter separates intimate friends. (Prov. 17:9)

If we seek to love others, then Solomon would tell us we must learn to forgive. That's what it means to "conceal" a transgression.

---

3. Archibald Thomas Robertson, *Word Pictures in the New Testament* (Grand Rapids, Mich.: Baker Book House, 1931), vol. 4, p. 178.

4. Curtis Vaughan and Thomas D. Lea, *1 Corinthians*, Bible Study Commentary Series (Grand Rapids, Mich.: Zondervan Publishing House, Lamplighter Books, 1983), p. 136.

However, if we choose to retaliate by "repeating a matter," then even our closest friendships won't last long.

Love Does Not Take into Account a Wrong Suffered

Imagine a ledger in which business transactions are recorded for proof and easy recall—that's the idea Paul was conveying here. Love keeps no ledger of wrongs done; it harbors no grudges. Instead, love forgives (see Matt. 18:21–35; Eph. 4:32). Spiros Zodhiates put it this way: "Love does not permit the evil that is flung at us to become imbedded in our memory."[5]

Two Principles to Live By

The information on love—and its resulting implications—is starting to stack up. We've covered nine characteristics so far, and we've got six more to go. Let's pause now and consider again how we can apply the truths about love to our own lives. As we seek to become more loving, it will be tremendously helpful to keep two principles in mind.

First, *never underestimate the enduring impact of love.* The following story removes all doubt:

> A college professor had his sociology class go into the Baltimore slums to get case histories of 200 young boys. They were asked to write an evaluation of each boy's future. In every case the students wrote, "He hasn't got a chance." Twenty-five years later another sociology professor came across the earlier study. He had his students follow up on the project to see what had happened to these boys. With the exception of 20 boys who had moved away or died, the students learned that 176 of the remaining 180 had achieved more than ordinary success as lawyers, doctors and businessmen.
>
> The professor was astounded and decided to pursue the matter further. Fortunately, all the men were in the area and he was able to ask each one, "How

---

5. Spiros Zodhiates, *To Love Is to Live* (Grand Rapids, Mich.: William B. Eerdmans Publishing Company, 1967), p. 134.

do you account for your success?" In each case the reply came with feeling, "There was a teacher."

The teacher was still alive, so he sought her out and asked the old but still alert lady what magic formula she used to pull these boys out of the slums into successful achievement.

The teacher's eyes sparkled and her lips broke into a gentle smile. "It's really very simple," she said. "I loved those boys."[6]

Godly love, without a doubt, can have an enduring impact on the lives of those who receive it.

Second, *always remember that love breaks down barriers that nothing else can.* Jesus, in love, broke down the "dividing wall" between Jews and Gentiles (Eph. 2:11–22), prevailing over all forms of racial and ethnic divisions. With love, we can tear down the racial "pride" that so often results in fighting and political posturing. With love, we can resist prejudice—*all forms of it.* And we can become people who reach out and build up others who possess different skin colors or cultural customs than our own.

More than that, love can break down barriers of all kinds, such as those caused by non-racial issues: competition, arguments, pride, rejection, and abuse. Remember, love covers a multitude of sins (1 Pet. 4:8). With love, we can build churches where people will find shelter from the hatred and apathy that are so rampant in the world around us.

If we constantly bathe our thoughts with these truths about *agape* and the principles that can help us apply them, never again will we shrug off the needs of others. Never again will we turn a blind eye to the pain and suffering of the persecuted and impoverished. In other words, never again will we allow the void of love in our lives to be filled with love's opposites—hatred *and* apathy. Rather, we'll fill ourselves with the Lord's love, and then pour it into others, just as God intended. People are looking for love. Let's make our churches places where they can find it.

---

6. Eric Butterworth, "Love: The One Creative Force" in *Chicken Soup for the Soul* (Deerfield Beach, Fla.: Health Communications, Inc., 1993), pp. 3–4.

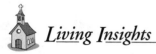 _Living Insights_

Love does not seek its own. What an alien concept in this "look out for number one" world. But Dr. Alan Loy McGinnis, in his touching and practical book, _The Friendship Factor_, provides a lucid example of one woman who lived to elevate another:

> Anne Sullivan gave most of her life to Helen Keller. When her famous pupil decided to go to college, she sat beside her in every class at Radcliffe, spelling out the lectures into Helen's hand and over-using her own defective eyes to spell out books that were not in Braille.
>
> Anne Sullivan recognized that Helen was a prodigy and had unlimited possibilities for thinking and feeling. There was no question as to which of the two had the higher IQ. By the time she was 10, Helen was writing to famous persons in Europe _in French_. She quickly mastered five languages and displayed gifts which her teacher never pretended to have.
>
> But did that change Anne Sullivan's devotion? Not so far as we know. She was satisfied to be Helen's companion and encourager, allowing her to be applauded by kings and presidents and to be her own unique personage.[7]

From the moment Anne helped deaf and blind Helen unearth the dazzling jewel of communication, the teacher committed her life to helping her pupil shine.

God hasn't called all of us to be Anne Sullivans. But He does expect us to demonstrate the others-centeredness aspect of His love. We sometimes focus so much on ourselves that we're blind to the daily opportunities we have to help others meet _their_ needs and achieve _their_ dreams.

This Living Insight is adapted from "It's Not a Meal Without Love" in the Bible study guide _Koinōnia: A Recipe for Authentic Fellowship_, written by Gary Matlack, from the Bible-teaching ministry of Charles R. Swindoll (Anaheim, Calif.: Insight for Living, 1995), pp. 15–16.

7. Alan Loy McGinnis, _The Friendship Factor_ (Minneapolis, Minn.: Augsburg Publishing House, 1979), p. 61.

Before you feel overwhelmed, realize that very few expressions of love require the time and energy displayed by Anne Sullivan. Sometimes we just need to listen. Or suggest a way for someone to use his or her gifts. Or discuss a topic that interests your friend or spouse instead of always talking about *your* favorite subject. Imagine what would happen if more employers took an interest in what their employees wanted out of life. Or if employees genuinely cared about the success of their superiors and the vision of the company or ministry. What if we devoted as much energy to learning about others' needs as we do to listing our own demands?

Look around. See anybody who could benefit from an expression of your love? Jot down their names.

_____

_____

What, specifically, can you do to show them *agape* love?

_____

_____

_____

_____

_____

_____

You never know. You just might be the light that helps someone else see more clearly . . . and succeed more completely.

Chapter 13

Unfailing Qualities of Christlike Living

Romans 12:1–2; 1 Corinthians 13:6–8a

Having made it to the last stretch of Paul's description of love, you've probably noticed a glaring difference between his version of love and the world's. Movies, soap operas, and hit songs usually present love as a self-satisfying, often sexual venture. Sitcoms and talk shows advocate quick fixes for relationships, downplaying long-term commitment and sacrifice. The world rarely defines love as what we give—it is more concerned with what we get.

How different the Lord's blueprint is from the world's defective diagram! As Paul has shown us, God's way of loving lifts people up; it spends more time smiling at the bright side of people's lives than it does scowling at the dark. It encourages the good in others instead of nitpicking the bad. Christlike love is an others-centered, service-minded commitment. It affirms and builds up. It stays off the arrogant throne of judgment and follows Jesus' gentle heart instead.

Now, Jesus knows that loving others with God's love does not come naturally to us. Left to our own devices, we tend to love as the world does. What we need is to be transformed so that our minds think like Christ thinks. Paul addressed this very need in Romans 12. Let's go there to gain a deeper understanding of what it means to be a transformed person. Then we can finish looking with Paul at love—the fruit of a transformed life.

Our Need to Be Transformed

Paul began by highlighting a contrast: being conformed to the world versus being transformed into Christlikeness.

> Therefore I urge you, brethren, by the mercies of God, to present your bodies a living and holy sacrifice, acceptable to God, which is your spiritual service of worship. And do not be conformed to this world, but be transformed by the renewing of your mind, so that you may prove what the will of God is, that which is good and acceptable and perfect. (Rom. 12:1–2)

With a sense of urgency, Paul called us to consecrate ourselves to God as a living sacrifice—everything we are and have are to be given to God in service to Him (v. 1). In order to be a holy and acceptable sacrifice, we need to do two things.

First, we need to *refuse to be conformed to this world*—not thinking as the world thinks, doing as it does, or loving as it loves. In other words, not living by the world's blueprint. We are not to adopt the external, fleeting, shallow superficiality of our ever-changing culture and its fads and fashions. As J. B. Phillips phrased it, "Don't let the world around you squeeze you into its own mould" (v. 2).

The second and more positive thing we are to do is *be transformed by the renewing of our minds,* or as Phillips puts it:

> Let God re-make you so that your whole attitude of mind is changed. (v. 2a)

To be transformed means to have deep-seated change take place where we make decisions, form opinions, and shape our perspectives about life and other people. How are we transformed, then? By the *renewing* of our minds. In another of his epistles, Paul described the renewing process like this:

> Finally, brethren, whatever is true, whatever is honorable, whatever is right, whatever is pure, whatever is lovely, whatever is of good repute, if there is any excellence and if anything worthy of praise, dwell on these things. (Phil. 4:8)

Dwell on these things, the apostle tells us. In our relationships, this means seeing the true, honorable, and lovely in people. When our attention is fixed on God's redemptive power and His grace in others' lives, then we know our minds are being made new and we are being transformed.

Isn't it interesting that Paul shifted from speaking about transformation (Rom. 12:1–2) to how we fit and relate with others (vv. 3–8), and finally to the theme that ties it all together: love.

> Let love be without hypocrisy. (v. 9a)

We are never more Christlike than when we love another individual unconditionally. As Ray Stedman once noted: "It is not our relationship *with* Jesus Christ which counts before the world, it is our resemblance *to* him."[1] We can only make an eternal impact on the world and its people when we walk in the same way of love that Christ did.

Love in Action

Let's rejoin Paul in 1 Corinthians 13, where we'll learn seven more characteristics of active, Christlike love.

Does Not Rejoice in Unrighteousness

Christlike love does not find delight in another's fall but seeks their good. Commentator David Prior observes,

> There is a perverse streak in human nature, played on and pandered to by most communicators, which actually enjoys evil, particularly in others. We can fall into the trap of rejoicing, not in what is good and true, but in the murky and sordid. We find false solace in seeing others fail and fall, presumably because we imagine it gives us more leeway to trifle with sin ourselves. That is the reverse of love, which longs to see others stand and grow, which is saddened and hurt when another is defeated.[2]

Love also does not lead another person into sin. We need to be wary of the phrase, "If you really love me, you will . . ." This kind of manipulation is driven by selfishness, not love. Real love never leads a person to demand sex as proof of devotion. Nor does it drive televangelists to siphon money from naïve viewers. Christlike love, remember, denies self-gratification and seeks to serve the highest and best for others.

Rejoices with the Truth

That petite but potent preposition *with* tells us that love and truth are partners; they go hand in hand. Wherever you find love, you'll find truth. If you love someone, you'll be up-front with him or her—even if it creates discomfort (see Prov. 27:6). Love doesn't

---

1. Ray C. Stedman, *Talking to My Father: What Jesus Teaches About Prayer* (Portland, Ore.: Multnomah Press, 1975), p. 122.

2. David Prior, *The Message of 1 Corinthians: Life in the Local Church*, The Bible Speaks Today Series (Downers Grove, Ill.: InterVarsity Press, 1985), p. 232.

play games, doesn't compromise, doesn't spread gossip, and doesn't lie. And it certainly doesn't believe that truth is "relative"; that is, that truth is whatever people perceive it to be. No—truth is absolute, and there are moral absolutes. The Bible is the foundation for truth, whether our culture accepts this or not. True love is based on the idea that there are right and wrong ways to treat people. *Agape* rejoices with the truth.

Bears All Things

Paul began his "all things" list (v. 7) with *bears all things*. In the New Testament, the verb translated *bear* was used only by Paul. It is rendered *endure* in other passages (1 Cor. 9:12; 1 Thess. 3:1, 5). His meaning here, however, is probably closer to "love 'covers' all things," which reflects the root meaning of the verb—"to cover, to conceal."[3]

Don't misunderstand; Paul wasn't suggesting that love operates with deceit or stealth, like a shady politician. Rather, love overlooks wrong done to it. Whether it is attacked, misunderstood, unappreciated, or betrayed—love doesn't stop to lick its wounds. It keeps going.

Believes All Things

"Believes *all* things"? Did Paul mean we must become gullible to practice *agape*? Not at all. Remember, love dwells in the realm of the truth. Discernment, wisdom, weighing options—all these can and should coexist with love. *Believe*, in the Greek, means "trust." Love is trusting, not suspicious. Commentator Alan Redpath illustrates love's trust this way:

> [Love] takes the kindest view of others in every circumstance, as long as it possibly can. Love will consider the motives and make every allowance for failure. And when a man has fallen, love will think about the battle that he must have fought, and the struggle that he must have had before he went down.[4]

Love gives the benefit of the doubt.

---

3. Gerhard Kittel and Gerhard Friedrich, eds., *Theological Dictionary of the New Testament*, translated and abridged by Geoffrey W. Bromiley (1985; reprint, Grand Rapids, Mich.: William B. Eerdmans Publishing Co., 1992), p. 1073.

4. Alan Redpath, *The Royal Route to Heaven: Studies in First Corinthians* (Westwood, N.J.: Fleming H. Revell Co., 1960), p. 166.

Hopes All Things

The word *hope* usually brings to mind wishful thinking: "I hope I win the lottery." "I hope Bob's not mad at me." "I hope Megan remembers to feed the goldfish." But the biblical concept of hope goes beyond wishful thinking to *confident expectation*. Ernst Hoffmann asserts, "In the New Testament [hope] never indicate[s] a vague or fearful anticipation, but always the expectation of something good."[5]

Paul used the term frequently to urge believers to focus on future events—our ultimate perfection, Christ's second coming, and so on—that are absolute certainties based on God's faithfulness (see Gal. 5:5; Col. 1:4–5; Titus 2:13). Hope for the Christian, then, grows from our faith in a God who keeps His word.

So, what did Paul mean when he said love "hopes all things"? That love always believes the best about people? More likely, he meant that love always believes the best about *God's ability to work in people's lives*. How dismal our churches would be if we had no hope that people could change—that we could grow more dependent on Christ, clean up our language, get the upper hand on a bad habit, or learn to appreciate our spouse. Love never loses hope. It believes that the Potter's hand still shapes souls.

Endures All Things

Love perseveres; it never gives up. A. T. Robertson says love "carries on like a stout-hearted soldier."[6] You can shoot at love, deprive it of comfort and recognition, even launch an ambush against it. But it keeps on marching, long after events and emotions tell it to stop. Does that mean we let others walk all over us like a welcome mat? Certainly not. But it does mean that love keeps going. How can it not, since our God always does?

Love Never Fails

Finally, love never ends (1 Cor. 13:8a). Unlike prophecy, tongues, and knowledge, which will all pass away (v. 8b), love will go on forever: "It will never fold under pressure, but will continue on through

5. Ernst Hoffmann, "Hope," in *The New International Dictionary of New Testament Theology*, ed. Colin Brown (Grand Rapids, Mich.: Zondervan Publishing House, Regency Reference Library, 1986), vol. 2, p. 241.

6. Archibald Thomas Robertson, *Word Pictures in the New Testament* (Grand Rapids, Mich.: Baker Book House, 1931), vol. 4, p. 179.

death into eternity."[7] Why will *agape* last? Because it's indomitable; it never falls and is never brought to the ground.[8] Never.

When we love people with *agape*—Christ's unfailing love—we tend to be less disturbed when people treat us poorly, such as when the boss makes false assumptions about us, our spouses take us for granted, or our friends exclude us. Why? Because our focus is no longer on ourselves. We're committed to serving and loving God and others, regardless of the response—just like Christ did.

> One will hardly die for a righteous man; though perhaps for the good man someone would dare even to die. But God demonstrates His own love toward us, in that while we were yet sinners, Christ died for us. (Rom. 5:7–8)

 Living Insights

Remember what we said about love at the beginning of this chapter: it spends more time smiling at the bright side of people's lives than it does scowling at the dark. In other words, love encourages. And amazing things happen when we lift others up with the power of positive words, as the story of one woman shows.

> Jean Nidetch, a 214-pound homemaker desperate to lose weight, went to the New York City Department of Health, where she was given a diet devised by Dr. Norman Jolliffe. Two months later, discouraged about the 50-plus pounds still to go, she invited six overweight friends home to share the diet and talk about how to stay on it.
>
> Today, 28 years later, one million members attend 250,000 Weight Watchers meetings in 24 countries every week. Why was Nidetch able to help people take control of their lives? To answer that, she tells a story. When she was a teenager, she used to cross a park where she saw mothers gossiping while the

---

7. Prior, *The Message of 1 Corinthians*, p. 233.

8. Gerhard Friedrich, ed., *Theological Dictionary of the New Testament*, trans. Geoffrey W. Bromiley (Grand Rapids, Mich.: William B. Eerdmans Publishing Co., 1968), vol. 6, p. 166.

toddlers sat on their swings, with no one to push them.

"I'd give them a push," says Nidetch. "And you know what happens when you push a kid on a swing? Pretty soon he's pumping, doing it himself. That's what my role in life is—I'm there to give others a push."[9]

That's the loving Christian's role too—to give pushes of encouragement to people when they need them. Who do you know who could really use some encouragement?

_____

_____

How can you build this person up? To discern this, first look at what is causing the discouragement. Is it a lack of confidence? Fear? Feeling like no one cares? Failure? Unexpected setbacks? Weariness? Try to be specific regarding this person's needs.

_____

_____

_____

_____

Encouragement comes in all shapes and sizes—it's not a "one size fits all" kind of action. In fact, it often involves a mixture of some of the following qualities:

sensitivity	kindness	gentleness
consideration	softness	humility
empathy	friendliness	tenderheartedness
cheerfulness	care	compassion
openness	respect	trust
vision	appreciation	grace

What do you think would most encourage the person you have thought of? A warm hug or tender touch? A cheering word or gentle smile? Try to gear your encouragement toward their needs, personality, and how they best receive input from others. For example,

9. Irene Sax, Newsday, accessed June 13, 2000: available at http://www.sermonillustrations.com/newpage173.htm.

some people are not the touchy-feely type but more shy and reserved, so a bear hug will probably leave them shaken instead of shored up. Likewise, people who thrive on affection may get more of a lift from an arm around their shoulders than a pep talk. Keep it natural for them—and for you too!

_____

_____

_____

_____

_____

_____

_____

_____

As important as it is to encourage others, it's also essential to let others know when you need encouragement. Sometimes we need to be like the little boy who said to his dad, "Let's play darts. I'll throw, and you say, 'Wonderful!'"[10]

Do you need encouragement right now? God doesn't want you to bear your burdens alone. Who can you share your heart with? Choose someone you can trust, who can love you with *agape*. And remember, we always have an ultimate Comforter—God Himself. We can come to Him anytime in prayer, because He Himself has encouraged us to cast our burdens on Him and rest in His care (see 1 Pet. 5:7).

As you seek to live a life of receiving God's love and encouragement and passing it on to others, remember the power God has put in this kind of life:

> Encouragement is awesome. Think about it: It has the capacity to lift a man's or woman's shoulders. To spark the flicker of a smile on the face of a discouraged child. To breathe fresh fire into the fading embers of a smoldering dream. To actually change

10. *Bits and Pieces*, December 9, 1993, p. 24, accessed June 13, 2000: available at http://www.sermonillustrations.com/newpage173.htm.

the course of another human being's day . . . or
week . . . or life. . . .

Is it easy? Not on your life. It takes courage,
tough-minded courage, to trust God, to believe in
ourselves, and to reach a hand to others. But what
a beautiful way to live. I know of no one more needed,
more valuable, *more Christ-like*, than the person who
is committed to encouragement. In spite of others'
actions. Regardless of others' attitudes. It is the mu-
sical watchword that takes the grind out of living—
encouragement.[11]

11. Charles R. Swindoll, *Encourage Me* (Portland, Ore.: Multnomah Press, 1982), pp. 85–86.

Chapter 14

THE CHURCH THAT *REALLY* LIVES

1 Thessalonians 3:8–13

Cotton Fitzsimmons used to coach in the NBA. One year, his team was performing poorly and was seated at the bottom of the league standings. Suffering from discouragement and a lack of confidence, they found themselves in the midst of a long, intense losing streak. Coach Fitzsimmons, in an effort to break through their mental block, gave the team some strange advice:

> "I want you to think about one word: pretend. It's a new word for us. Pretend we're not losers. Let's pretend we are winners. Pretend we're not on a losing streak; pretend we're on a winning streak. Pretend we're not at the bottom; pretend we're at the top. Pretend this is not just your basic basketball game in the middle of the season; pretend this is the last game of the playoff series, and if we win it, pretend that we win the crown. We get it all."[1]

The men took their coach's directions, confidently ran onto the basketball court, and with stern determination in their eyes, soundly lost the game.

The story, however, does not end there. Back in the locker room afterward, Coach Fitzsimmons sat dejected on a bench. The room was stifled in silence, the players waiting for their coach to speak, and he not knowing what to say. Finally, one of the players broke the silence. "Cheer up, coach," he said. "Just pretend we won!"

The moral to this story? Pretending rarely helps solve real problems. For example, pretending that you're not deep in debt won't erase your balance if you've purchased thousands on your credit card. Nor does pretending you're a doctor qualify you to perform surgery. And pretending that you're healthy won't save you from a serious illness.

In a similar way, pretending does no good for churches, especially when it comes to gauging their spiritual health. How do you

---

1. Source unknown.

measure the strength of a church? How can you tell if one is living or dying? A basketball team can know if it's winning or losing by looking at the scoreboard. A doctor can tell if a patient is well or sick by looking at an X-ray or blood test. Evaluating a church, on the other hand, is a much more subjective process.

Thankfully, we're not left on our own to make that determination. The apostle Paul, in his first letter to the Thessalonians, modeled for that congregation four observable "vital signs" of a believer—and a church—that *really* lives.

Four Vital Signs

Paul founded the Thessalonian church, yet he was only able to stay with them a short time. Because he was unable to return to them (1 Thess. 2:18), he sent Timothy to visit them and bring him a report. The update had quite an impact on the apostle:

> But now that Timothy has come to us from you, and has brought us good news of your faith and love, and that you always think kindly of us, longing to see us just as we also long to see you, for this reason, brethren, in all our distress and affliction we were comforted about you through your faith; for now we really live, if you stand firm in the Lord. (3:6–8)

Paul stated that he *really lived* if the Thessalonians stood firm in their faith. Because Timothy's report indicated that they were doing just that, Paul responded with great joy, modeling the first vital sign of a healthy Christian life—joy and gratitude. It was an attitude that he wanted all believers in all churches to possess.

Joyful in an Attitude of Gratitude

> For what thanks can we render to God for you in return for all the joy with which we rejoice before our God on your account? (v. 9)

Paul thanked God for the great joy he experienced over the news of the Thessalonians' steadfast faith and love for him. His feelings were not merely a shallow, circumstance-based happiness, but ran much deeper than that. Did you notice, for example, his reference to "distress and affliction" in verse 7? Commentator John Stott explains the grave danger Paul had encountered as a result of his relationship with the Thessalonian church:

Jealous of Paul's influence in the city, the Jews recruited a gang of thugs and started a riot. Not finding Paul or Silas in Jason's house, where they were staying, the ringleaders dragged Jason and some other believers before the city magistrates (whom Luke correctly calls 'politarchs') and lodged a serious accusation against them: 'These men who have caused trouble all over the world have now come here, and Jason has welcomed them into his house. They are all defying Caesar's decrees, saying that there is another king, one called Jesus.' This allegation threw the city into an uproar. Jason and his friend were put on bail, and that night under cover of darkness Paul and Silas had to be smuggled out of town.

They went south to Berea for a short mission. But the Jews followed them there, so that Paul had to continue his southward journey to Athens, where his escort left him.[2]

Despite the need to run for his life, Paul still rejoiced and thanked God for the Thessalonians. He succeeded in his example because they, too, showed that they could hold on to joy in the face of great persecution. In fact, one of the terms Paul used to describe his own situation, *affliction*, he also used of their predicament.

> You also became imitators of us and of the Lord, having received the word in much *tribulation* with the joy of the Holy Spirit. (1:6, emphasis added)

Although *affliction* is translated *tribulation* here, the Greek word behind the English, *thlipsis*, is the same. Despite their hard times, the Thessalonians still found joy—the joy of the Holy Spirit. But was their joy deep, like Paul's? To find out, let's take a look at the intensity of the tribulation they faced.

> [*Thlipsis*] denotes not mild discomfort, but great and sore difficulty. The Jews who stirred up a riot against Paul (Acts 17:5) and followed him to Berea (Acts 17:13) would not have left the new converts

2. John R. W. Stott, *The Gospel and the End of Time: The Message of 1 and 2 Thessalonians* (Downers Grove, Ill.: InterVarsity Press, 1991), p. 18.

unmolested, and there was further opposition from the local pagans (1 Thess. 2:14). There is every reason for thinking that the Thessalonian Christians had been sorely tried.[3]

The Thessalonians were getting persecution from both sides—from the Jews *and* the pagans—yet they continued to overflow with the joy of the Holy Spirit. Paul's example was leading them to become a church that really lived.

Earnest in the Practice of Prayer

Paul next showed them that life in the body must also include earnest prayer:

> Night and day we pray most earnestly that we may see you again and supply what is lacking in your faith. (3:10 NIV)

In these few words, Paul provided the Thessalonians, and us, with a gold mine of information about how to pray. First, he revealed that prayer must be *frequent:* he prayed "night and day." Now, those who have read the whole epistle will perhaps stop right here and scratch their heads wondering, "Didn't Paul just say that he *'worked* night and day'? How could he do both at the same time?"

Paul did say that very thing in chapter 2, verse 9. He was able to do both simultaneously because he prayed *as* he worked. He was a mature believer who spoke to the Lord spontaneously and silently while he did other things. He didn't have to wait for a church service or a small group meeting to talk to his Lord. He did it by himself all the time. And this is what he meant when he told the church of Thessalonica to "pray without ceasing" (1 Thess. 5:17).

In addition to praying night and day, he also prayed *earnestly.* Let's not skim past this thought. *Earnestly* is a special adverb used exclusively by Paul to describe the highest form of effort imaginable.[4] He used it to describe God's immeasurable and limitless power in Ephesians 3:20: "Now to Him who is able to do *far more abundantly* beyond all that we ask or think, according to the power that works within us . . . ." (emphasis added).

---

3. Leon Morris, *The First and Second Epistles to the Thessalonians,* rev. ed., The New International Commentary on the New Testament Series (Grand Rapids, Mich.: William B. Eerdmans Publishing Co., 1991), p. 48.

4. Morris, *First and Second Epistles to the Thessalonians,* p. 105.

How often do we pray with "far more abundant" effort? was the last time you broke a sweat during prayer—when you p so intently that you completely forgot about your circumstanc surroundings? It's this kind of fervent prayer of which Paul spe and it's this kind that infuses our churches with vitality.

Finally, Paul modeled for us prayer that is *specific*. What, spe cifically, did he request of the Lord for the Thessalonians? That he would see them again and "supply" (NIV) or "complete" (NASB) what was "lacking" in their faith (v. 10). "Complete," *katartizo* in the Greek, means to "restore, equip, or complete."[5] It's used of a fish-erman repairing his nets, a surgeon setting a bone, a politician reconciling factions, and a Christian helping his or her fellow be-lievers overcome sin (see Gal. 6:1). Paul prayed that he would be able to complete the Thessalonians' faith by filling in whatever gaps they had in their knowledge or practice.

What better way to illustrate his thoughts on prayer than to provide an example? This is exactly what Paul did.

> Now may our God and Father Himself and Jesus
> our Lord direct our way to you. (1 Thess. 3:11)

Paul still sought to visit his fellow believers in Thessalonica, but until he was able to do so, he was content to continue teaching them via the written word.

Abounding in a Life of Love

Paul continued his prayer and, in doing so, revealed a third characteristic of spiritual vitality:

> And may the Lord cause you to increase and abound
> in love for one another, and for all people, just as
> we also do for you. (v. 12)

If you want to know how important love is to church life, just remind yourself that we spent four chapters covering 1 Corinthians 13:1–8. That comes out to about two verses per chapter—love is no small matter! Remember all the attributes we looked at? The key, Paul stated here, is to keep increasing and abounding in those traits. Dying churches are not only those that become infested with hatred and infighting but also those in which the members simply stop loving each other.

5. Stott, *The Gospel and the End of Time*, p. 66.

,ure that our love continues to increase and
measure of a successful church is not the size
eauty of its campus. Rather, it's how well the
other, forgive one another, listen to one another,
for each other, and reach out to those in need

,hed in a Heart of Holiness

,ly, Paul concluded his prayer and revealed one more vital
a church that really lives:

> So that He may establish your hearts without blame
> in holiness before our God and Father at the coming
> of our Lord Jesus with all His saints. (1 Thess. 3:13)

When describing God, *holiness* means pristine, pure, uncontaminated. We, of course, cannot attain to that level of purity until God transforms us and gives us new bodies in heaven. But we can become, as Paul says, "without blame." Ray Stedman explains:

> *Unblamable* does not mean sinless, as we have already seen; *unblamable* means dealing with what is wrong, not covering it up or pretending it is not there. The Thessalonian Christians dealt with sin in their hearts with the spiritual resources provided by God, and thus were enabled to turn from evil and walk closer and closer with the Father.[6]

Now, we can do that, can't we? Actually, we can't. Look more closely at Paul's prayer. He said, "so that *He* may establish your hearts without blame" (emphasis added). God does the establishing, not us. He is the One who will be faithful to complete the good work He began in us (see Phil. 1:6). He will give us the strength to grow and mature while we're on this earth.

A church that really lives is one that is filled with believers whose hearts are established in holiness. It's a priority to them. In fact, it's so much of a priority that they're willing to be accountable for it. Just seven questions can help keep us on track:

1. Have you been with a member of the opposite sex anywhere this past week that might have been viewed as compromising?

6. Ray C. Stedman, *Waiting for the Second Coming: Studies in Thessalonians* (Grand Rapids, Mich.: Discovery House Publishers, 1990), p. 57.

2. Have any of your financial dealings lacked integrity?

3. Have you sought out any sexually explicit material since we last met?

4. Have you spent adequate time in the study of Scripture and in prayer?

5. Have you given priority time to your family and their needs?

6. Have you fulfilled the mandates of your vocation and your calling?

7. Have you just lied to me?

Is there room for pretending in the church? Absolutely not. We can't pretend our way into joy when, in reality, our attitudes have soured. We can't pretend to be serious about prayer because our real lives will betray us. Love, too, cannot be pretended without the telltale clanging of cymbals giving us away. And we can't pretend that we have no sin by sweeping our problems under the church carpet. If we do, we might as well call Coach Fitzsimmons to be our pastor—and expect similar results.

However, if we choose to get serious about joy, prayer, love, and holiness, we'll become people who *really* live, and our churches will become *really* alive!

 Living Insights

Have you ever ordered something over the phone? If you have, you know how comforting it is to have the sales representative read your order back to you.

"Okay, ma'am. You want six pairs of jeans with the tapered-leg cut and button fly, model number EB51LV."

"Yes."

"And you want them all 28 waist, 31 inseam. Three pairs in the acid-washed color and three in stonewashed. Correct?"

"That's right."

"Your order is in the computer. It should go out tomorrow, and you'll get your jeans in three days. Thank you for shopping with Mail Order Jeans Company."

If we need details on something as garden-variety as a jeans order, how much more do we need details on the life-changing matter of prayer!

Unfortunately, when we tell family and friends, "I'm praying for you," we usually leave out exactly what we're praying for.

Did you notice what Paul did? He not only told the Thessalonians the specifics of his prayers for them, but he actually wrote his prayer out for them to read! What an encouragement that must have been.

Let's follow Paul's example. Below, jot down the name of a friend or family member whom you have been praying for; then use the space provided to practice writing out the specifics you hope to see God accomplish in his or her life. And don't forget to share it with them!

Name: _____

Practice prayer: _____

_____

_____

_____

_____

_____

_____

_____

_____

_____

_____

_____

_____

Chapter 15
THE ALL-IMPORTANT ROLE OF SERVANTHOOD
Acts 6:1–7; 1 Timothy 3:8–13

Some people just don't know what to do with Christians. When they find out a person is "religious," they often stop cussing in midstream, try not to exhale their cigarette smoke, hide their drinks behind their backs, and blush at their own dirty jokes. They stiffen up, become unnaturally formal, and restrict their conversations to safe subjects like the economy or how to keep weeds from sprouting in the lawn.

Some, though, take the opposite tack and assume that being "religious" is the same as being "holier-than-thou." They sarcastically label Christians "Goody-Two-shoes" or "Preacher." The more creative ones try titles like "friar" or "deacon."

That last term, *deacon*, however, doesn't come close to meaning "holier-than-thou"—it actually refers to a "humbler-than-thou" person. In Greek, the word is *diakonos*, meaning "servant."[1] Serving others as Christ did is at the heart of Christianity, so labeling Christians with this title unwittingly sums up the truth about who they are.

Why is serving so central to Christianity? And how did the specialized office of deacon—an ordained servant—come about? Let's search for the answers by examining what the Bible has to say about serving and servanthood.

What Does It Mean to "Deacon"?

Being called a servant doesn't sound like much of a compliment, does it? In the eyes of most people today, it isn't. Neither was it to many people in biblical days:

> In Greek eyes serving is not very dignified. Ruling

Parts of this chapter have been adapted from "The Dignity of Servanthood" in the Bible study guide *Excellence in Ministry: A Study of 1 Timothy*, written by Gary Matlack, from the Bible-teaching ministry of Charles R. Swindoll (Anaheim, Calif.: Insight for Living, 1996).

1. Walter Bauer, *A Greek-English Lexicon of the New Testament and Other Early Christian Literature*, 2d ed. Revised and augmented by F. Wilbur Gingrich and Fredrick W. Danker, from Walter Bauer's 5th ed., 1958 (Chicago, Ill.: University of Chicago Press, 1979), p. 184.

and not serving is proper to a man. . . . The formula of the sophist: "How can a man be happy when he has to serve someone?" expresses the basic Greek attitude. . . . Logically, the sophist argues, a real man should simply serve his own desires with boldness and cleverness.[2]

Things haven't changed much over the centuries, have they? Servanthood is still seen as degrading and something to avoid. For Christians, though, servanthood is not a sign of inferiority or weakness. Rather, it's one of the ways in which we "descend into greatness." We don't need to look any further than the New Testament to see that. Consider Christ Himself and the very reason He came:

> "For even the Son of Man did not come to be served [diakoneo], but to serve [diakoneo], and to give His life a ransom for many." (Mark 10:45)

Christ's example influenced those who knew Him. Look at what Scripture says about some of the women who followed Him:

> When He was in Galilee, they used to follow Him and minister [diakoneo] to Him; and there were many other women who came up with Him to Jerusalem. (Mark 15:41)

These women may have looked after Jesus' and the disciples' physical needs as they did the work of the ministry. If so, they certainly knew how Jesus felt about servanthood. Perhaps they even recalled these words of His:

> "Truly, truly, I say to you, unless a grain of wheat falls into the earth and dies, it remains alone; but if it dies, it bears much fruit. He who loves his life loses it, and he who hates his life in this world will keep it to life eternal. If anyone serves [diakoneo] Me, he must follow Me; and where I am, there My servant [diakonos] will be also; if anyone serves [diakoneo] Me, the Father will honor him." (John 12:24–26)

2. Gerhard Kittel, ed., *Theological Dictionary of the New Testament*, trans. and ed. Geoffrey W. Bromiley (1964; reprint, Grand Rapids, Mich.: William B. Eerdmans Publishing Co., 1993), vol. 2, p. 82.

Diakoneo is frequently used to describe ideal Christian behavior —behavior that pleases God and will be richly rewarded by Him. We're most like His Son, Jesus Christ, when we're serving people with His love.

The First Deacons

Since servanthood is such a high priority in the life of faith, it's no surprise that an official position was created in the church to ensure that the physical needs of the body are met. Interestingly, it was a problem over meeting these needs that instigated the formation of deacons.

> Now at this time while the disciples were increasing in number, a complaint arose on the part of the Hellenistic Jews against the native Hebrews, because their widows were being overlooked in the daily serving of food. So the twelve summoned the congregation of the disciples and said, "It is not desirable for us to neglect the word of God in order to serve tables. Therefore, brethren, select from among you seven men of good reputation, full of the Spirit and of wisdom, whom we may put in charge of this task. But we will devote ourselves to prayer and to the ministry of the word." The statement found approval with the whole congregation; and they chose Stephen, a man full of faith and of the Holy Spirit, and Philip, Prochorus, Nicanor, Timon, Parmenas and Nicolas, a proselyte from Antioch. And these they brought before the apostles; and after praying, they laid their hands on them. (Acts 6:1–6)

The Hellenistic widows were hungry, and the ministry of food distribution called for someone to attend to their needs. But the apostles, who were acting as overseers, needed to stay focused on their primary ministry of prayer and teaching the Word.

So the apostles had the congregation select seven men to serve tables (vv. 2–3). These men became the first deacons, a transliteration of the word *diakonos*. They weren't looked down upon; on the contrary, they were highly esteemed. How do we know this? First, notice the qualifications decreed by the apostles—a good reputation, full of the Holy Spirit, and wise. Can anyone head up a service ministry? The apostles didn't think so. They wanted responsible, godly, honest people to oversee the meeting of others' needs.

Consider also the results of their ministry. The widows were fed. Members of the body experienced the joy of serving one another. The prayer and teaching ministry of the apostles continued without interruption. And the church retained its reputation as a caring community. All this because seven men became servants.

By the time Paul wrote to the Philippians, the role of deacon had broadened beyond the first seven men to become an office in the church (see Phil. 1:1). Local assemblies had recognized the need for an official ministry that met the physical needs of the congregation and allowed the elders to focus on spiritual leadership.

Since servanthood is important, so important that an official position was created for it, let's look at the qualifications someone must meet to hold the office.

Four Qualities of Deacons

In 1 Timothy 3:8–13, Paul supplied a list of qualifications for deacons. All are necessary when evaluating a person for the office, but each of us can develop these qualities to become more godly in our service.

> Deacons likewise must be men of dignity, not double-tongued, or addicted to much wine or fond of sordid gain, but holding to the mystery of the faith with a clear conscience. These men must also first be tested; then let them serve as deacons if they are beyond reproach. . . . Deacons must be husbands of only one wife, and good managers of their children and their own households. (vv. 8–10, 12)

Dignity

First, deacons are people of *dignity*. They have a high standard of conduct. Their behavior is not frivolous, shallow, superficial, or silly. This doesn't mean they don't have any fun or possess a sense of humor. But they should demonstrate determination, commitment, and stability. As a result, they are respected by others.

They are respected, for one reason, because they have verbal integrity—they're *not double-tongued*. Commentator William Barclay explains that

118

[the Greek word] *dilogos* means *speaking with two voices*, saying one thing to one and another to another. . . . A deacon, in his going from house to house, and in his dealing with those who needed charity, had to be a straight man. Again and again he would be tempted to evade issues by a little timely hypocrisy and smooth speaking. But the man who would do the work of the Christian Church must be straight.[3]

This phrase also suggests that deacons keep confidences. In the scope of their service, they will be trusted with information from other church members, much of which is sensitive and secret. Deacons should be trustworthy and discerning enough to know what to keep and what to share.

Deacons should also *not be addicted to much wine*. A person under the influence of alcohol can't adequately serve the body, have clear, Christlike thinking, or model God-honoring behavior. As God's servants, we can't seek to dull our senses and escape from life; rather, we must be tuned in, present, and keenly aware of life's challenges and people's pain—including our own.

Finally, deacons should *not be fond of sordid gain*. Commentator William Hendriksen explains the meaning of this qualification.

A man who is fond of money is not necessarily an embezzler. But it is the embezzler or pilferer and the man who joins a good cause for the sake of material advantage whom Paul has in mind here in verse 8. It is the man with the mercenary spirit who goes all out in his search for riches, anxious to add to his possessions regardless of the method, whether fair or foul.[4]

Deacons, and all who desire to serve others in a Christlike way, need to be people of dignity.

Orthodoxy

Deacons must also be people who *hold to the mystery of the faith with a clear conscience* (v. 9). In other words, they are deeply spiritual

3. William Barclay, *The Letters to Timothy, Titus, and Philemon*, rev. ed., The Daily Study Bible Series (Philadelphia, Pa.: Westminster Press, 1975), pp. 85–86.

4. William Hendriksen, *Exposition of I and II Thessalonians*, New Testament Commentary Series (Grand Rapids, Mich.: Baker Book House, 1955), p. 131.

believers who embrace and exemplify the orthodox beliefs of Scripture. A. Duane Litfin describes it this way:

> They should be men who understand and hold fast the deep truths of the faith. By the phrase *"with a clear conscience"* Paul (cf. "good conscience" in 1 Tim. 1:5) meant that there must be nothing in the conduct of these men that was glaringly inconsistent with their professed beliefs. In other words they must not profess one thing but practice another. (emphasis added)[5]

God's Word changes lives, and He wants servants who show evidence of that change. You see, God doesn't just want to plug warm bodies into church programs. He wants living, breathing models of His revealed truth.

Maturity

Paul commanded that deacons be *tested* before they're approved (v. 10). The Greek word for test, *dokimazo*, means "to test in the hope of being successful."[6] Paul wasn't describing a squint-eyed scrutiny fueled by suspicion, but he was urging an observation with the anticipation of approval. One commentary further explains that testing

> refers not to some formal testing but rather to observation by those who appoint deacons. The candidate will have shown the required moral characteristics and approved doctrine (3:9) consistently in the ordinary activities of church membership. A man who has proven his quality over time can then serve as a deacon. Testing deacons is needed today. They should not be appointed without consideration of their doctrine and their Christian life.[7]

Deacons have to do more than fill a slot and pass the plate. They must prove their maturity by passing the test.

5. A. Duane Litfin, "1 Timothy," in *The Bible Knowledge Commentary*, New Testament edition, ed. John F. Walvoord and Roy B. Zuck (Colorado Springs, Colo.: Chariot Victor Publishing, 1983), p. 738.

6. Donald Guthrie, *The Pastoral Epistles* (Grand Rapids, Mich.: William B. Eerdmans Publishing Co., 1990), p. 96.

7. Bruce B. Barton, David R. Veerman, and Neil Wilson, *1 Timothy, 2 Timothy, Titus*, Life Application Bible Commentary Series (Wheaton, Ill.: Tyndale House Publishers, 1993), p. 68.

Fidelity

Finally, deacons must be people of fidelity (v. 12). They must be loyal to their spouse—as Paul said, the men should be *husbands of only one wife*. Also, these servants must show faithfulness to their whole families by being *good managers of their children and their own households*.

As with elders, the measuring stick of good management is found in the home, not a business. A deacon who exercises authority with love, wisdom, orderliness, and a servant's heart will bring those same qualities to the church.

Women . . . Likewise

Let's not forget what Paul said to the women in this passage:

> Women must likewise be dignified, not malicious gossips, but temperate, faithful in all things. (v. 11)

Paul used the term *gyne,* which is translated both "women" and "wife" in the New Testament.[8] To whom, then, does verse 11 apply? Is Paul referring to (1) the wives of deacons, (2) all women in the church, or (3) female deacons—deaconesses?

The third option seems to have the most merit for several reasons. First, notice the term *likewise.* Paul used this word to link items in a series (compare with v. 8). In this context, Paul was dealing with positions in the church. It seems natural that he would include deaconesses along with elders and deacons, rather than dealing with women in general.

Second, the pronoun *their* is conspicuously absent in the Greek text. It seems that Paul would have spoken of "their wives" if he were referring to the spouses of deacons.

Finally, Scripture contains several examples of women who served faithfully in the early church. Consider, for example, Phoebe (Rom. 16:1), Priscilla (v. 3), and Lydia (Acts 16:14–15). The record of these women's vital contributions and lifestyles may point to the office of deaconess.[9]

8. Gerhard Kittel and Gerhard Friedrich, eds., *Theological Dictionary of the New Testament,* translated and abridged into one volume by Geoffrey W. Bromiley (Grand Rapids, Mich.: William B. Eerdmans Publishing Co., 1985), p. 134.

9. This is a debated issue. Some scholars believe this passage allows for only males to hold the office of deacon.

Deaconesses, then, are held to the same standard of character as deacons. Their conversations and lifestyles must reflect the qualities of a mature believer.

The Rewards of Servanthood

What can servants such as deacons and deaconesses expect in return for their years—and even decades—of quiet, faithful service? Thunderous applause? Rarely. High visibility? Not usually. No, their reward is much greater than human accolades:

> For those who have served well as deacons obtain for themselves a high standing and great confidence in the faith that is in Christ Jesus. (1 Tim. 3:13)

A. Duane Litfin illuminates this verse for us:

> Though the position of deacon seems by worldly standards to be menial and unattractive, to close followers of Jesus Christ it looks quite different. . . . Those who fulfill their servant roles faithfully gain two things: first, an excellent standing before fellow Christians who understand and appreciate the beauty of humble, selfless, Christlike service; and second, great assurance . . . in their faith in Christ Jesus. Humble service, which lacks all the rewards the world deems important, becomes a true test of one's motives. [10]

Because the world does not understand us, they'll always call us names like "Goody-Two-shoes," "Reverend," or even "deacon." That's okay; let 'em do it. It's a title of dignity and worth—a title Christ Himself chose. Can we aspire to anything higher?

 Living Insights

As we've already noted, you don't have to hold the office of deacon to serve. Some people serve the body as teachers, pastors, elders, or staff members. Others serve by singing in the choir, greeting

---

10. Litfin, "1 Timothy," p. 738.

visitors, or maintaining the church grounds. All of us, though, should be serving the body to some degree. That's why the church is called "the body of Christ." We're all interconnected; every part has something to offer that will benefit the whole.

Are you currently serving in some way in your local church? If not, why?

_____

_____

_____

_____

What are the most pressing needs in your church community? What's most often listed in the bulletin or newsletter?

_____

_____

_____

Have you prayed and asked God what He would like you to do? Is He leading your heart in a certain direction? Spend some time talking to Him about this, asking Him to show you what He'd like you to do. What is He telling you?

_____

_____

_____

_____

What can you do this week to begin serving His body?

_____

_____

Now, don't hesitate. Become a servant today!

Chapter 16

STAYING FOCUSED ON CHRIST

1 Timothy 3:14–16

Well, we've covered a wealth of information, haven't we? The Master's plan for His church has included such priorities as qualifications for leaders, ways to engage our surrounding culture, and especially the expressions of Christlike love, just to name a few. These are all worthy and essential priorities to pursue, but in the midst of them, we don't want to lose sight of our highest priority: Jesus Christ.

You see, the Christian faith isn't a do-gooders' club—though doing good for the glory of God is part of our mission. It's not just a cultural crusade—though being salt and light in our world is part of our calling. It's not a system of dos and don'ts—though reflecting God's righteousness is part of our charge.

Christianity, and the church, is about *Christ*—loving Him, listening to Him, following Him, and serving Him. He is our everything. As Paul wrote in his letter to the Romans, "For from Him and through Him and to Him are all things" (11:36). So when we take our eyes off of Him, whatever we do—no matter how well-intentioned—will amount to nothing (see John 15:4–5; Rev. 2:2–4). It is essential that we live an active faith together, but it must be a faith that mounts up on the eagle's wings of Christ's grace. As the writer to the Hebrews put it,

> Let us run with perseverance the race marked out for us. Let us fix our eyes on Jesus, the author and perfecter of our faith, who for the joy set before him endured the cross, scorning its shame, and sat down at the right hand of the throne of God. (Heb. 12:1b–2 NIV)

As we rejoin Paul in 1 Timothy, we'll find an appropriate finale to our study of Christ's church in a hymn of exaltation to our Lord and Savior, Jesus Christ.

Honoring Christ in Our Conduct

Service done in Christ's name, as we learned in our last chapter, has to come from a life aligned with God's values (1 Tim. 3:1–13). Dignity, self-control, gentleness, faithfulness—these qualities should distinguish the Christian servant. Paul had no doubt talked about this to his protégé, Timothy, but he wanted to put it in writing for his young friend just in case he couldn't personally teach him in more depth.

> I am writing these things to you, hoping to come to you before long; but in case I am delayed, I write so that you will know how one ought to conduct himself in the household of God, which is the church of the living God, the pillar and support of the truth. (vv. 14–15)

Paul's phrase "how one ought to conduct himself" means much more than not fidgeting in church or knowing when to stand, sit, or kneel. The word *conduct, anastréphō* in Greek, includes such ideas as "to act, to walk."[1] It describes a person's

> whole life and character; but it specially describes him in his relationships with other people. . . . A church member's personal character must be excellent. . . . A church congregation is a body of people who are friends with God and friends with each other.[2]

Why is our behavior so important? Because we belong to "the household of God, which is the church of the living God, the pillar and support of the truth" (v. 15). These phrases give rich descriptions of our identity and responsibility in Christ. Let's delve into each one and savor its meaning.

The Household of God

Because of our redemption in Christ, we have become members of God's own household. The apostle John explained,

> As many as received Him, to them He gave the right to become children of God, even to those who believe in His name, who were born, not of blood nor of the will of the flesh nor of the will of man, but of God. (John 1:12–13; see also 1 John 3:1a)

Once we were rebellious enemies of the Lord, but now, by the

---

1. Gerhard Kittel and Gerhard Friedrich, eds., *Theological Dictionary of the New Testament*, translated and abridged in one volume by Geoffrey W. Bromiley (1985; reprint, Grand Rapids, Mich.: William B. Eerdmans Publishing Co., 1992), p. 1094.

2. William Barclay, *The Letters to Timothy, Titus, and Philemon*, rev. ed., The Daily Study Bible Series (Philadelphia, Pa.: Westminster Press, 1975), p. 88.

atoning work of Christ, we've been transformed into His dearly loved children (see Rom. 5:6–11; 8:15–16). We're in His family, members of His household. This means that we have relationships with other members of the household as well as with the Master of the house. Philip H. Towner shows what Paul's image reveals about the church:

> The concept of household with its associated notions of interdependence, acceptable conduct and responsibility was so strong that Paul could borrow it to illustrate the nature of the church. It too, both then and now, is made of different groups (men and women from every level of society, parents and children, employers and employees) who must depend upon and, in love, serve one another, and it is the task of the stewards (bishops/elders, deacons) to ensure that the household accomplishes the Master's goals.
>
> . . . If by our commitment to one another we can even approximate the ideal of unity and cooperation traditionally connected with the household, we will present to the unbelieving world an attractive alternative lifestyle.[3]

The church, then, is not a corporation, not a program, but a tightly-knit family. God is our Father, not the chairman of the board; Jesus is our brother, not our CEO. And Jesus is the One who has opened the door and invited us in to become God's household, "the church of the living God" (1 Tim. 3:15).

The Church of the Living God

As the Lord's church, the assembled people of the living God, we are a unique community.[4] The Lord has called us out from the world—from sin and hopeless estrangement—to be distinct in holiness and purpose. And we know that His calling is sure, because He is the *living* God. He is

> the eternal, ever-living One
> > the Giver of life
> > > the Conqueror of death
> > > > the ever-present One

3. Philip H. Towner, *1–2 Timothy and Titus*, The IVP New Testament Commentary Series (Downers Grove, Ill.: InterVarsity Press, 1994), pp. 94–95.

4. The Greek word for *church, ekklēsia,* means "assembly" or "congregation."

126

Not even the grave could keep Jesus' love from us (Rom. 8:31–39). And with His return to the Father, the Spirit makes His home with us and indwells us (1 Cor. 3:16). Unlike the distant deadness of pagan deities, the Lord is alive and active, more near to us than we can know.

How should we conduct ourselves as the church of the living God?

> The privilege of being called out to live in God's presence carries with it . . . the responsibility to live a life worthy of the One who has called. God's calling of the Hebrews out of Egypt into association with himself required them to be holy (Lev. 11:45); and membership in the church of the living God makes the same demand (compare 1 Pet. 1:15–16).[5]

Because our Lord is holy, we, His household, are called to celebrate and uphold holiness—we testify to the majestic reality of God.

The Pillar and Support of the Truth

"I am the way, and the truth, and the life," Jesus told us, "no one comes to the Father but through Me" (John 14:6). By His sacrificial death on the cross, Christ secured for us the forgiveness of sins and reconciliation with God the Father. This is the gospel of our salvation, the word of truth we are to "pillar" and "support" (1 Tim. 3:15). What do these two images tell us about our responsibilities as Christ's church? John Stott explains that

> the purpose of pillars is not only to hold the roof firm, but to thrust it high so that it can be clearly seen even from a distance. . . . Just so, the church holds the truth aloft, so that it is seen and admired by the world.[6]

In addition to proclaiming the gospel, we're also called to "support" it, or as William Barclay phrases, to "buttress" it:

> The buttress is the support of the building. It keeps it standing intact. In a world which does not wish to face the truth, the Church holds it up for all to see. In a world which would often gladly eliminate

5. Towner, *1–2 Timothy and Titus*, p. 95.

6. John Stott, *Guard the Truth: The Message of 1 Timothy and Titus* (Downers Grove, Ill.: InterVarsity Press, 1996), p. 105.

unwelcome truth, the Church supports it against all who would seek to destroy it.[7]

Preserving the purity of the gospel of Jesus Christ against the contamination of false teaching, as well as keeping its pristine beauty unmarred by sinful conduct that would discredit it, is absolutely crucial. Why? Because there is no other way to eternal life but through Jesus Christ. As Peter said,

> "There is salvation in no one else; for there is no other name under heaven that has been given among men by which we must be saved." (Acts 4:12)

Our lives should open the way to Christ for others and keep that way clear of anything that would block it. And we can only do this when our own way to Christ is clear, not strewn with well-intentioned distractions or worthy diversions. Too often we let good things block us from the best; even things like service and clean living can deflect us from our calling when we forget *why* we serve and lead moral lives. The *why* that Paul didn't want Timothy or us to forget is Jesus Christ, whom Paul turned our eyes toward in an excerpt from one of the church's earliest hymns.

Refocusing on Christ through Our Remembrance

"By common confession," Paul wrote,

> Great is the mystery of godliness:
> He who was revealed in the flesh,
> Was vindicated in the Spirit,
> Seen by angels,
> Proclaimed among the nations,
> Believed on in the world,
> Taken up in glory. (1 Tim. 3:16)

"By common consent" (or as the NIV renders Paul's words, "beyond all question"), how immense is the secret plan of God revealed to us in Christ—this is what "the mystery of godliness" is. The word *mystery*, *mysterion* in Greek, denotes

> the eternal counsel of God which is hidden from the world but eschatologically fulfilled in the cross

---

7. Barclay, *The Letters to Timothy, Titus, and Philemon,* p. 89.

of the Lord of glory and which carries with it the glorification of believers. . . . The *mystērion* embraces the historical enactment of God's purpose.[8]

God's purpose has been fulfilled in Christ's death and resurrection —this was God's hidden plan of salvation from the beginning of time. Jesus has taken away our sins and given us His righteousness, which makes it possible for us to be godly (see Rom. 3:21–26).

To recount all that Christ has done for us, Paul quoted part of a well-known hymn of that day, each phrase of which provides a snapshot of Jesus' life and ministry. Let's look at what each picture tells us.

He who was revealed in the flesh focuses our attention on Jesus' Incarnation. This reminds us that He humbly set aside heaven's glories to take on a human body. Being both truly God and truly man, He was subject to fatigue, sadness, pain, and even death. How great is the love that would stoop so far to save!

Was vindicated in the Spirit turns our eyes toward the supernatural proofs Jesus gave through the Spirit's power, which affirmed that He was truly the One He claimed to be. The miracles Jesus performed, the people He healed, and the power of His Resurrection all proved that He was God's chosen One and that His promises were true. Through His Resurrection, Christ triumphed over His enemies, over Satan, and over death itself.

Seen by angels reminds us of the joyful proclamation of the angelic host at Jesus' birth, their aid to Him after His wilderness temptation, their message to His friends and disciples at His empty tomb, and their eternal songs of praise that resound in heaven. He who created the angels was "made for a little while lower than the angels" (Heb. 2:9), but with our salvation secured, He returned to His exalted state and now rules on the throne of His glory.

Proclaimed among the nations reveals "the universal scope of the gospel. It is not restricted to the Jews but is for the Gentiles also."[9] Though He came to the house of Israel first, Jesus still reached out to a Roman centurion and a Samaritan woman. And the Good News of salvation in Jesus Christ spread from Jerusalem, then to all Judea, then to the formerly excluded Samaritans, and it continues to reach out to the uttermost parts of the earth (see Acts 1:8).

8. Kittel and Friedrich, *Theological Dictionary of the New Testament*, p. 617.

9. Ronald A. Ward, *Commentary on 1 and 2 Timothy and Titus* (Waco, Tex.: Word Books, Publisher, 1974), p. 66.

Christ broke down all the barriers that keep people apart and brought us together to be one in the Father (see Eph. 2:11–22). As Paul noted in Galatians, even the barrier of our differences falls away in Christ:

> There is neither Jew nor Greek, there is neither slave nor free man, there is neither male nor female; for you are all one in Christ Jesus. (Gal. 3:28)

Believed on in the world shows us the ever-expanding mural of redemption that is being created worldwide through those who have placed their faith in Christ. Not only has Jesus been proclaimed throughout the world, but He has been believed on by people from every portion of the globe. Interestingly, "*the world* is characterized by its hostility to God. Here then in the hymn the church sees enmity turned into faith."[10] Those who were once God's enemies have become His beloved children by trusting in Christ.

Taken up in glory is the climax that directs us to Jesus' Ascension, where His suffering was over and He was once again exalted at the right hand of His Father. Christ released His glory at the Incarnation, but He has now returned to that glory, where

> at the name of Jesus every knee will bow, of those who are in heaven and on earth and under the earth, and . . . every tongue will confess that Jesus Christ is Lord, to the glory of God the Father. (Phil. 2:10–11)

What pictures of grace, love, and hope we have to look at! And what a gracious, loving, encouraging Lord we have to gaze on! Why would we ever want to take our eyes off of Him?

A Concluding Thought

What happens, then, when we gaze on Jesus, meditate on His life, and focus on His heart? As we've seen in Romans 12, our minds are renewed and we're transformed (v. 2). Our perspectives and pursuits are transformed—like Zaccheus, we care more about compassion and integrity than getting wealthy at the expense of others (see Luke 19:1–9). And our views and values are transformed— like Peter, we can let go of our prejudices and embrace others with God's expansive love (see Acts 10).

10. Ward, *Commentary on 1 and 2 Timothy and Titus*, p. 66.

Transformation doesn't come through programs, formulas, or lists of rules. Those things merely compel us to conform outwardly; they don't touch and change a heart—only a person can do that. Jesus Christ is that Person, and it's His life pulsing through His body, the church, that makes it alive and vital.

So in all that you do, keep your eyes fixed on Jesus. He's our reason for being and our motivation for living. If we hold fast to Him, there's no telling what we can accomplish in His name!

 Living Insights

How fitting for our study on the Master's plan for the church to conclude with a chapter on Jesus Christ. After all, He's the head and heart and life of our body. Everything we think and do ought to revolve around Him, because without Him, as without love, we are nothing. As He told us Himself,

> "Abide in Me, and I in you. As the branch cannot bear fruit of itself unless it abides in the vine, so neither can you unless you abide in Me. I am the vine, you are the branches; he who abides in Me and I in him, he bears much fruit, for apart from Me you can do nothing." (John 15:4–5)

Let that last phrase sink in: "For apart from Me you can do *nothing*" (emphasis added). No matter what programs we initiate, no matter how hard we try to "do church" right, nothing we attempt without putting Christ at the center of it will have any eternal value.

Have you ever tried to do great things for God but found that somehow Christ was getting left out of it? What were you attempting? What happened as a result?

_____

_____

_____

_____

_____

_____

What caused you to take your eyes off of Christ? What had to happen to bring your focus back to Him?

_____

_____

_____

_____

Of the areas we have studied in our guide—prayer, leadership, service, engaging culture, evangelism, vision, and love—which one do you often find yourself trying to do in your own power? Why?

_____

_____

_____

How does focusing on Christ change what you do? For example, how does He impact your motives, attitudes, and responses? What difference does putting Him in charge make in how you handle problems and conflicts?

_____

_____

_____

_____

As you strive to build your church according to the Master's plan, remember why you're doing what you do and for whom you're doing it. As Paul reminded us,

> You are no longer strangers and aliens, but you are fellow citizens with the saints, and are of God's household, having been built on the foundation of the apostles and prophets, Christ Jesus Himself being the corner stone, in whom the whole building, being fitted together, is growing into a holy temple in the Lord, in whom you also are being built together into a dwelling of God in the Spirit. (Eph. 2:19–22)

BOOKS FOR PROBING FURTHER

T hough we've taken a long, thoughtful look at God's blueprints for the church, many more details remain to be drawn out. If you want to learn more about His design for body life—His priorities, plans, and desires—the following bibliography can help extend your study. May these resources enable you to sketch out the details in accordance with the Architect's design!

Anderson, Leith. *A Church for the 21st Century*. Minneapolis, Minn.: Bethany House Publishers, 1992.

Fagerstrom, Douglas L., and James W. Carlson. *The Lonely Pew: Creating Community in the Local Church*. Grand Rapids, Mich.: Baker Book House, 1993.

Frye, John W. *Jesus the Pastor*. Grand Rapids, Mich.: Zondervan Publishing House, 2000.

Guinness, Os. *Dining with the Devil: The Megachurch Movement Flirts with Modernity*. Grand Rapids, Mich.: Baker Book House, 1993.

Laney, J. Carl. *A Guide to Church Discipline*. Minneapolis, Minn.: Bethany House Publishers, 1985.

Liesch, Barry. *People in the Presence of God: Models and Directions for Worship*. Grand Rapids, Mich.: Zondervan Publishing House, 1988.

Logan, Robert E., and Larry Short. *Mobilizing for Compassion: Moving People into Ministry*. Grand Rapids, Mich.: Baker Book House, Fleming H. Revell, 1994.

Ortiz, Manuel. *The Hispanic Challenge: Opportunities Confronting the Church*. Downers Grove, Ill.: InterVarsity Press, 1993.

Petersen, Jim. *Church Without Walls*. Colorado Springs, Colo.: NavPress, 1992.

Peterson, Eugene H. *The Contemplative Pastor: Returning to the Art of Spiritual Direction*. Grand Rapids, Mich.: William B. Eerdmans Publishing Co., 1993.

————. *Under the Unpredictable Plant: An Exploration in Vocational Holiness.* Grand Rapids, Mich.: William B. Eerdmans Publishing Co., 1992.

————. *Working the Angles: The Shape of Pastoral Integrity.* Grand Rapids, Mich.: William B. Eerdmans Publishing Co., 1993.

Schaller, Lyle E. *Looking in the Mirror: Self-Appraisal in the Local Church.* Nashville, Tenn.: Abingdon Press, 1984.

Stedman, Ray C. *Body Life.* 3d ed. Ventura, Calif.: Gospel Light Publications, Regal Books, 1979.

Stevens, R. Paul. *Liberating the Laity: Equipping All the Saints for Ministry.* Downers Grove, Ill.: InterVarsity Press, 1985.

Swindoll, Charles R. *The Bride: Renewing Our Passion for the Church.* Grand Rapids, Mich.: Zondervan Publishing House, 1994.

————. *Improving Your Serve: The Art of Unselfish Living.* Dallas, Tex.: Word Publishing, 1981.

Towns, Elmer L. *An Inside Look at 10 of Today's Most Innovative Churches: What They're Doing, How They're Doing It and How You Can Apply Their Ideas in Your Church.* Ventura, Calif.: Gospel Light Publications, Regal Books, 1990.

————. *10 Sunday Schools that Dared to Change: How Churches across America are Changing Paradigms to Reach a New Generation.* Ventura, Calif.: Gospel Light, Regal Books, 1993.

Yancey, Philip. *Church: Why Bother?* Grand Rapids, Mich.: Zondervan Publishing House, 1998.

Some of these books may be out of print and available only through a library. For those currently available, please contact your local Christian bookstore. Books by Charles R. Swindoll, as well as some books by other authors, may be obtained through Insight for Living.

Insight for Living also offers study guides on many books of the Bible, as well as on a variety of issues and biblical personalities. For more information, see the ordering instructions that follow and contact the office that serves you.

NOTES

NOTES

NOTES

NOTES

Ordering Information

The Master's Plan for the Church

If you would like to order additional study guides, purchase the cassette series that accompanies this guide, or request our product catalogs, please contact the office that serves you.

United States and International locations:

Insight for Living
Post Office Box 69000
Anaheim, CA 92817-0900

1-800-772-8888, 24 hours a day, seven days a week
(714) 575-5000, 8:00 A.M. to 4:30 P.M., Pacific time, Monday to Friday

Canada:

Insight for Living Ministries
Post Office Box 2510
Vancouver, BC, Canada V6B 3W7

1-800-663-7639, 24 hours a day, seven days a week
infocanada@insight.org

Australia:

Insight for Living, Inc.
20 Albert Street
Blackburn, VIC 3130, Australia

Toll-free 1800 772 888 or (03) 9877-4277, 8:30 A.M. to 5:00 P.M., Monday to Friday

World Wide Web:

www.insight.org

Study Guide Subscription Program

Study guide subscriptions are available. Please call or write the office nearest you to find out how you can receive our study guides on a regular basis.